Cevere's Chronicles
Volume 2:
Cevere's Classics

MARQUIS WALKER

www.TrueVinePublishing.org

Cevere's Chronicles Vol. 2

Marquis Walker

Published by True Vine Publishing Co.

810 Dominican Dr.

Nashville, TN 37228

www.TrueVinePublishing.org

Copyright © 2023 by Marquis Walker

All rights reserved. No part of this book may be reproduced in any form or by any electronic or mechanical means, including information storage and retrieval systems, without permission in writing from the publisher, except by a reviewer who may quote brief passages in a review.

ISBN: 978-1-7375934-9-2 Paperback

ISBN: 978-1-956469-86-8 eBook

Printed in the United State of America—First Printing

Table of Contents

Introduction:	7
Chapter 1: It's A Compton Thing	9
Chapter 2: Descendants of Cain	15
Chapter 3: God Level	20
Chapter 4: The Fix	23
Chapter 5: The Great Adventures of Slick Rick	29
Chapter 6: Ready to Die	35
Chapter 7: Reasonable Drought	42
Chapter 8: The Allegory	46
Chapter 9: Illmatic	50
Chapter 10: Livin' Like Hustlers	54
Chapter 11: The Score	59
Chapter 12: Muddy Waters	66
Chapter 13: Reasonable Doubt	73
Chapter 14: Only Built 4 Cuban Linx...	79
Chapter 15: Act Like You Know	86
Chapter 16: Last Chance, No Breaks	93
Chapter 17: Jewelz	99
Chapter 18: Sittin' on Chrome	105
Chapter 19: Strictly Business	111
Chapter 20: Street Cinema	116
Chapter 21: Dirty Harriet	121
Chapter 22: Stunts, Blunts, & Hip Hop	127
Chapter 23: Moment of Truth	134

Chapter 24: Hell on Earth 141
Chapter 25: Somethin' to Blaze To 146

Visit Cevere's Blog and Youtube Channel

Hip-hop Saved my Life

Blog

Marquis "Cevere" Walker

Youtube Channel

Introduction

Albums serve as a way for artists to present their music in a more complete and organized manner, allowing for a more immersive and cohesive listening experience. They often follow a particular theme or concept, and the songs are arranged in a deliberate order to create a specific flow or narrative.

A classic album refers to a musical album that is widely recognized and esteemed for its enduring quality, influence, and impact on the music industry or popular culture. Classic albums are considered to be exceptionally well-crafted, groundbreaking, or representative of a particular era or genre.

The term "classic" is subjective and can vary depending on personal tastes and cultural contexts. They embody various qualities that contribute to their status, including innovative production techniques, exceptional songwriting, memorable melodies, thought-provoking lyrics, influential performances, cultural relevance, and a lasting impact on music as a whole.

CHAPTER 1:
IT'S A COMPTON THING (FEBRUARY 1990)

Compton is known for N.W.A., Kendrick Lamar, and The Game, right? Of course, it is, but if you do your hip-hop homework, CMW is one of the first groups that represented. I bet if I said MC Eiht, you would say, "I know him." Well, he started off in a GROUP called "Compton's Most Wanted" aka CMW, and guess what, there's not one curse word in the entire project. This album was fully produced by T. Allen, D.J. Slip, and Big Beat Productions.

Compton's Most Wanted consisted of MC Eiht, Tha Chill, DJ Unknown, and DJ Slip. Eiht and Chill were the rappers, and of course, Unknown and Slip were the DJs/Producers. They also owned record labels back then, which were unheard of. To my knowledge, DJ Unknown owned Techno Hop Records, and Slip owned the biggest DJ renting company back then. Unknown brought a mixtape of Eiht and Chill to Slip, and history was made.

This group fell under the radar on most radio stations back in the day, and they would never have formed a group if it wasn't for their good friend MC Ren. Former N.W.A. member MC Ren back in those days got the word around about the group. Without social media, it was word of mouth, and you had to be good.

Marquis Walker

Eiht and Chill started making underground mixtapes and stopped allegedly gang banging. When they started circulating around the neighborhood, their music got in the right hands and was heard by people with good hearing.

The album is labeled Explicit, but it was for only the content of gangster rap and not the actual words said. The group never swore – not in one song. They bleeped out swears, scratched over them, and silenced them during the entire record. Even without swears, this album is more gangster than albums now with every other word being a curse or the "N" word.

I'm not sure why they never swore, but it worked for me. I didn't even notice to be honest until a friend mentioned it to me. If you know why they didn't curse, please let me know. Was it a record label thing? Did the artist choose not too? And while I'm asking questions, did Eiht write this entire album? There are rumors he wrote for Tha Chill. I need someone to verify this.

I was aware that Tha Chill got locked up for joyriding so he couldn't complete the album. That's why you hear more of MC Eiht. Chill continued this pattern of going to jail and not completing the next two albums as well. This is why I believe MC Eiht became a solo artist eventually.

Every time I write Eiht, I want to add the "G" and so does Microsoft correction. And the reason I mention this is because if you remember, Eiht and DJ Quik used to have real beef. Like, 'I'm going to kill you' beef.

Cevere's Chronicles Vol. 2

But they kept their beef on wax the majority of the time, and every time I think of the wrong way of the spelling of Eight, I think of one of DJ Quik's verses from a track called "Dollaz + Sense." Quik says, "Giving your set a bad name with your misspelled name/E-I-H-T, now should I continue? /Yeah, you left out the G 'cause the G ain't in you". That was a hard bar. Sorry Eiht, it's just a part of hip-hop.

Let's get back to this album. The production seemed like a smooth 70's-style mix honoring groups like EPMD's style. It was smooth and melodic. Beats that you take with those long showoff trips with your boys to impress the ladies. The production is baby-butt smooth. And if some of the tracks didn't have DJ cuts in them, you wouldn't know it was an older-sounding album. On some of these albums, I will break down song for song and others, I'll just speak in paragraph form.

I'm Wit Dat

As soon as the track starts, you want to blast it out your stereo speakers at the highest volume. Then the beat drops and Eiht starts rapping and you just fall for that voice. Chill is just as smooth, and they sound alike a bit. They feed off each other and make the song hotter than cooked grits. The D.O.C.'s voice sample for the chorus gave it more flavor.

Marquis Walker

Final Chapter

This song is funkier than your underarms after you work out. The beat drops again and it's on like popcorn. The way the rappers flowed was just as effortless as the music released from the speakers. The scratching and mixing are classic, and Mc Eiht spit four verses on this song. There are rappers these days that only rap eight bars and be like, that's a song.

I Give Up Nuthin

Another musical gem right off the back. Eiht was dropping raps like they were running out of style. The music is just as important as the rhymes, giving us equal, level tracks. Eiht was passionate about his flow, and it went well with this western hip-hop track.

This Is Compton

After this track you wanted to be from Compton for sure. Chill is back with Mc Eiht and they are toasting this track with simple, but fly, bars. With the samples and scratches acting as the chorus, it brings an old school feel, but it still hits like Mike Tyson. Shoutout to the DJs on the cuts.

We Made It

They slow down the track a bit on this song to get in story mode. I'm so curious what "Chicken Bottle" is. It must be some malt liquor or liquor that puts you on your butt. I'm not cursing on this review, based on how they didn't on the album. It shows you can make quality rap without swearing or the use of the "N" Word. Both rappers put in work on this song. And if you notice, it's over six minutes. It's a song and album to just ride too. They made it.

One Time Gaffled Em Up

The music continues too just be good. They beep the curse words, and it still sounds great. And the samples and DJ are blessing the chorus as Mc Eiht says "F" the police in his own way. Eiht put in work on the microphone on this entire project. His stories, bars, and the actual substance he speaks are appreciated.

Duck Sick

This is a clever record to not curse on. Just switch the first two letters in each word in the title. "You can get my Duck Sick!" says Mc Eiht. The jazzy hip-hop tune is a highlight of the album and will have you quoting it to others. Just make sure you say this to people who've heard this record before. Don't want you to get Gaffled. The breaks are just as much a part of the record as the scratches and samples, which are appreciated. And guess what; you can get Cevere's Duck Sick. LOL!

Marquis Walker

Late Night Hype

DJ Unknown put in some quality work on this project. This R&B smooth, funky track got me bobbing the head and toe-tapping while Chill and Mc Eiht rap about some late-night hype. The vibe of this record made me wish I had a drop top to blast this in. If you're not grooving to this song, you may be a zombie. This is one of the first gangster albums that I'm sure other artists stole from and mimicked.

I Mean Biznez

They speed up the track with this band-like track and it means business. The bass and horns are highlights along with the DJ cuts. I'm sure MC Eiht and Chill studied EPMD prior to making this album. They have a good back and forth chemistry, and besides EPMD samples, they favor them a bit. There's nothing wrong with reinventing the wheel, just having different threads is the key. No biting allowed back in those days. And biting means stealing.

It's A Compton Thang

The record is just as clean and funky as the others. Back in the day, we had longer attention spans, and with smooth sounds like this coming out the speakers, I had this entire album on blast. Thank you CMW for putting out quality music and making a point not to curse.

CHAPTER 2
DESCENDANTS OF CAIN (MAY 2020)

"Got to be in grace first, to fall from it
That money chase birthed the fall summit
Was wasteful as big eyes and a small stomach
Funny used to call my friends money, I lost hundreds"
– Ka (Solitude of Enoch)

Don't read any further if you didn't go insane from that verse above. This artist and album is a PROBLEM! Hip-hop has changed consistently since it began. Maybe I shouldn't use the word changed. Hip-hop has expanded to include various styles of expressions and tones. And with Brownsville, NYC emcee/producer Ka's 7th album release, it proves that his format of blessing the MIC is unique.

There is so much music out there for our ears and we are so lucky to have it. I was recently introduced to Ka in 2020 from someone who viewed one of my YouTube reviews. Music fan Jersey McGee informed me about KA. Thank you, Sir. And if you have an artist that you think I'd like, please suggest them. And it doesn't have to be rap music.

This album is needed currently and will be relevant as long as there is racism. During this worldly epidemic,

Marquis Walker

religious differences, and love & hate, honesty is needed and welcomed. Ka delivers. And my ears, soul and heart are listening and appreciating his wordplay.

You know how they say things happen for a reason. Well, this album was delivered to me because I needed it. I was going through tough times. I'm pretty sure you've lost family members like I have. The coronavirus was and is limiting life in general, and things seem to be falling apart for lots of people. This album will help you cope and give you a bit of hope. I'd like to thank Brownsville native Ka early in this review for his messages and content. And not being afraid to speak the truth.

Now, is this album religious? The theme is, but it's not gospel rap at all. It's more like the hip-hop bible. This album has my fingers on the rewind button. The beats allow you to hear the artist from beginning to end based on many of them being drum-less. The tracks are simple, clear, and not over the top with bass or drums. And his lyrics are intricate, and some may need to be dissected and broken down to appreciate the art and information he's presenting.

Most of the production was done by KA himself. He's found his groove by producing his 7th album. Producers such as Preservation, Animoss and Roc Marciano also bless a few tracks, but KA's production is heavy. They fit his ability to teach who's listening about his personal struggles and continuous grapples with the world.

Cevere's Chronicles Vol. 2

On "Every Now and Then" he quotes, "Loved things I should have lusted, I rushed it, snubbed things I should have trusted". This was his first line going into this album. I was hooked and drawn in with his lyricism from the beginning to the end of the project.

The beats are on a slower tone and not the boom bap most people are looking for when it comes to hip-hop. But like I said earlier, the production allows you to appreciate the lyrics this intelligent artist is flowing. On "Patron Saints" Ka takes us on a journey explaining his role models and past interactions that allegedly led him to drug dealing. "I was raised to age a few years in a day, if not elite, didn't eat if you didn't pray. As much as I heal, had to deal, all my scars are here to stay, our senseis spent days peddling, our heroes sold heroin."

WOW! I'm speechless at times when I catch bars like this. And he is lyrical like this throughout the entire album. He said our senseis (masters) spent days selling drugs; this is why he allegedly went down that negative road. People only do what they know. What they are taught. And life has taught this KING to express himself in ways the hip-hop community will envy.

I could quote this lyrical genius all day, but I'll let you judge for yourself when your ears are soaked with his cadence.

People will say he reminds them of artists such as Roc Marciano, Stove God Cooks and Knowledge the Pi-

Marquis Walker

rate. Guess what? That's a compliment. And if you do your research, you'll find out Ka has been putting out some of the best underground hip-hop albums released in the 2010s. Check out 2016's *Honor Killed the Samurai* and 2018's *Orpheus vs. the Sirens*. Some of his greatest work besides this joint.

You can even go further back with Ka's 2012 *Grief Pedigree* or 2013 *The Night's Gambit* which proved and set his stamp on hip-hop. Go back and listen to this artist's work. His poetic lyrics and clever metaphors are worthy of your attention now and in the future.

I'll let you know ahead of time though - if you love lyrical wordplay, this artist will be in your top 10 by the end of the day. If you don't like slower production, you might not be in tune. Not that the production is not good, it's just not the boom bap most are used to. This artist takes you on a mission on each record. He's a teacher, a poet, a human that is living and is not scared to tell the truth. His lyrical ability alone is 5 Mics.

This artist can flow off the sound of streaming water it seems. I'm just so hypnotized by his lyrical content that the beats usually fall in the distance. I'm very intrigued by how this performer creates, and how his mind works. If someone knows if this artist writes or spits from the head, let me know. What I do know is, he's a firefighter. So, salute to a hero twice. Once for his dangerous job and second for his enlightening music.

Cevere's Chronicles Vol. 2

And as I speak of firefighters, shoutout to my cousin Antone McCatty. He's a great man and he's also a firefighter.

KA, if you're reading this review, THANK YOU Brother. Your work is getting me through ups and downs like the stock market and spreading hope through me. Your work is healing us from this cruel world.

Chapter 3

GOD LEVEL (NOVEMBER 2019)

GORDO! We lost a LEGEND, a soldier of pure hip-hop and a good man. A hip-hop GOD! A MAN that everybody knew was TOP 5, but never included him. Fred The Godson is God Level.

People in music say albums need at least 5 to 10 years to be classed as classics. When I hear quality music with quality speech, I'm not waiting for others to bow down. I've bowed down to this gentleman since his existence and he finally put together a quality project to be highlighted. That's not to say others weren't good, it's just this one stands out like your first gray hair.

He's categorized as an underground rapper. So, is he an underground legend? Whatever you think he is, he is a hip-hop angel now. So, condolences to his family and close friends.

The Heatmakerz blessed Mr. Godson with solid production and sounds that will have your speakers bleeding. And if you have records that rock with an MC that gets busy, what does that mean? It means a project that will live on like his spiritual presence.

The Heatmakerz have been reviving the careers of many underground stars. They did it with Jim Jones' album, "El Capo", and they've done it with this one.

Cevere's Chronicles Vol. 2

Let's talk about how lyrical Fred is and how he mirrored these tracks. He's bar for bar one of the best rappers that ever blessed the microphone. He's up there with Jay-Z, Big L, Nas, Jadakiss, The Notorious BIG, Fabolous, Rakim, Lloyd Banks, Pharoahe Monch, 38 Spesh, Kool G. Rap, Black Thought, etc.

On one of my first YouTube videos, I asked people to name 10 rappers that could go bar for bar with Fred. Guess what? Not many people could. The conversation is open again. Get in touch with me and let's talk about it. And don't start just naming rappers that had careers. I'm talking about artists who throughout their careers, shone on the mic with bars and something to say. Fred's music has substance, value, and grit.

The features on this album are insane. Out of the seven features, I was only aware of four out of the seven. Who do you like below?

Axel Leon (Rapper)
Jim Jones (Rapper)
Marc Scibilia (Singer)
38 Spesh (Rapper)
Benny The Butcher (Rapper)
Bobbi Storm (Singer)
Sweetest Voice (Rapper)

All the rappers go bar for bar with Fred. Do they out rap him? Not all of them. We can argue that maybe 38

Marquis Walker

Spesh or Benny did. The Sweetest Voice held her own on "Lebron & Serena". And if you haven't looked up Axel Leon yet, set a reminder to do so now. And check out the singers as well. They "sanging", not singing.

    I don't break down each record, but on some albums, it's not needed when the music blends well and the rapper is in tune throughout. I enjoyed this entire album - period. What is your favorite Fred the Godson project? I'm sure this one is in your top five.

    Again, Rest in Paradise Frederick Thomas. Condolences to your family and friends again. Thanks for your contribution to HIP-HOP.

Fact Checker News: Fred the Godson, real name Frederick Thomas was a rapper and songwriter from the Bronx, New York City. He released several mixtapes, blessed people's albums and singles with features and put out quality albums. Fred the Godson collaborated with some of the best in the game, including Meek Mill, Pusha T, and Jadakiss, among others.

    Tragically, Mr. Thomas passed away on April 23, 2020, at age 35, due to complications from COVID-19. His loss and untimely passing were significant to the rap community around the world. Thank you, God, for blessing us with one of your Gods.

CHAPTER 4
THE FIX (AUGUST 2002)

He is sometimes forgotten in the Best Emcee debates. The Houston rapper Scarface is never forgotten in my book. With about five classic albums under his belt and other albums just as close, he should never be dismissed when it comes to being one of the greatest in the debates.

This artist is amazing in his own right. He's been lyrical and bar-worthy since he was a member of the legendary group Geto Boys in the late 1980s. This album alone was played so much by me, I thought about selling that poison again. Not!

This album was his 7th release. This album was his 1st release on Def Jam South, which was founded in 1999 from Def Jam Recordings with founder Russell Simmons. Other artists on that platform were Ludacris, Disturbing the Peace, and Young Jeezy.

The Source Magazine was on point when they ranked it 5 Mics. Other music platforms ranked it either 4/5 or 8/10. In all, most reviewers knew this album was a problem. If you haven't heard it, please do your ears and soul a favor. Also, check out "Deeply Rooted" and "The Diary" albums, which I believe are also classics. What are the classic albums you appreciate from the

Marquis Walker

rapper Scarface? Find me on social media and let's have a discussion.

This body of work was pretty much held down by Mr. Jordan, but he did have some heavy features. Jay-Z and Beanie Sigel blessed the joint "Guess Who's Back". NAS blessed "In Between Us", and he even had songstresses Faith Evans and Kelly Price shine on a couple of songs.

If you're not aware, Scarface's name is Brad Jordan. Yes, another Jordan who is considered a GOAT of their profession.

This 2002 record was supposed to be followed up by an album called "The Habit" in 2010. That never happened. He did continue to put out work, but in my opinion, after "The Fix", I loved 2007's "M.A.D.E." and 2015's "Deeply Rooted".

In March of 2020, we found out that Brad Jordan was fighting for his life because he'd caught the coronavirus. Thank goodness he recovered and is still performing.

Prior to his illness, he announced he was only going to put out albums if they were with other greats such as Jay-Z, NAS, Black Thought, Pharoahe Monch, Kurupt, Eminem or Fabolous, to name a few I'd like to hear with him. I'm not sure what happened to those projects, but this Album was adored by me below.

Cevere's Chronicles Vol. 2

The Fix/Mike Dean: A short intro of a crackhead describing the fix. His fix.

Safe/China Black

This track is not safe; it has that New Orleans parade type vibe while Scarface unleashes his stampede of bars about financial and legal knowledge for the next generation. This track is dangerous and pleasing to the ears.

In Cold Blood/Kanye West

This is Face just being coldblooded with gangster rap. He's letting his enemies know that he doesn't play around in these mean streets. Kanye was a major plug back then for beats, and he laced Bradford with a couple.

Guess Who's Back ft Jay Z & Beanie Sigel/Kanye West

This song is just unfair for the game. Kanye is at his best on the boards, Jay Z is in his prime and Beanie's there with that rough edge. And Scarface put in work and matched his features. Guess who's back? I know the lyricists are back on this track. Can you imagine if Kanye rapped on this too? This would have been a top five posse cut. He does bless the chorus; we may have to call this a posse cut, which consists of four or more rappers on a song.

Marquis Walker

On My Block/Lee Stone & Nashiem Myrick

Y'all should already know this record right here, it's a double classic by itself. The stories Facemob spoke about his block in Houston made every hood say, "That's my block too!" This is one of Scarface's top 10 records throughout his career, period. Producer's Hitmen sampled "Be Real Black for Me", a 1971 duet by Roberta Flack and Donny Hathaway.

Keep Me Down/Nottz

Sounds like Nottz took Scarface to the country on this track and Mr. Facemob took it back to the streets. Scarface quotes, "I been praying for heaven, I been living in hell." It's the tale of people trying to keep him down while he's climbing to the top. Crabs in the barrel theory.

What Can I Do? Ft Kelly Price/T-Mix

You know when Scarface slows it down, it's going to have some deep-rooted lyrics. Those poetic words may bring a tear to the eyes. I call records like this, the "Smile" theme. If you heard his song "Smile" featuring Tupac, you get my drift. Shoutout to the legend Kelly Price for supporting the record with class and appeal.

Cevere's Chronicles Vol. 2

In Between Us ft Nas/Scarface, Lofey & Mike Dean

This is another record you just must turn up until the speakers bleed. Can you imagine if Scarface and Nas did an entire album? I'll be the first in line holding the line back, so they won't get between us. Let's not leave out Tanya Herron on the hook. She murdered it. The song, bridge and melody really hit your soul and the lyrics they school us.

Someday ft Faith Evans/The Neptunes

With the help of Ms. Evans and The Neptunes track, Scarface speaks on becoming one with God. This song hits the soul as well. Scarface's slower songs are different, and they always have messages about life that help you some way or another.

Sell Out/T-Mix

This record is for all the sellout artists in the industry. Scarface says it best with, "Now, this is for these niggas switchin' they shit, Prostituting theyself, trying to get them a hit." Love the production too. It bangs like when Crips & Bloods rode in their murderous days.

Heaven ft Kelly Price/Kanye West & T-Mix

I prefer when Scarface slows the track down and just speaks clearly with stories and rhymes that lean to help society. Kelly Price on the hook is singing her pretty

Marquis Walker

heart out. Even when Face rapped about religion, it didn't sound preachy, but I would say he's a hip-hop Pope.

I Ain't the One ft WC/Flip & Tony Pizarro

Ice Cube spoke to the females in his version. WC and Face speak to the brothers in the hood, letting them know they aren't the one. Shoutout to WC sticking to the script and adding value. Scarface lays down two verses to finalize he isn't the one or the two to be played with.

Fixed/Brad Jordan & Mike Dean:

This was just the outro to the intro. Sounds like the basehead got his fix from Scarface and now he's satisfied. And if this album is anything like hard drugs, I get my fix every time I listen. Thanks Scarface. "It keeps calling me!" - Chris Rock (Pookie)

Chapter 5
THE GREAT ADVENTURES OF SLICK RICK (NOVEMBER 1988)

The Ruler is Back! It's his debut album, so he was just actually beginning. Well, I'm back at least to go in the crates and bless y'all with another one like DJ Khalid. If you like storytelling, you will love this album. Mr. Rick has influenced so many rappers that you all know and love. He's your favorite rapper's favorite rapper.

Slick Rick is hands down one of the best storyteller rappers. He's always put out quality work. Check his discography and bow down to the ruler.

The fun part of doing these reviews is the memories that come back to me when I first listened. I'm sure you can relate to an artist you first heard of a while back. You tend to have somewhat of a connection with that artist. Maybe you relate to them based on what you're going through in life, or the music just gets you in the mood you prefer.

I notice that half the production was done by "The Bomb Squad", who are legendary producers. If you don't know who they are, it's the production crew behind hip-hop classic rappers like the group Public Enemy and Ice Cube's comeback after he divorced N.W.A. Their production was equal to any producer you are checking for currently. It was fresh, experimental, and just kicked butt.

Marquis Walker

When I first heard Mr. Rick, I fell in love with his voice and rhyme flow. He's a British rapper who was raised in the Bronx. No rapper had that distinct voice and storytelling capacity prior to him, and if they did, they weren't on my radar. This could be why people still to this day argue about whether he's one of the top five poets when it comes to stories.

Another reason I love digging in the crates and reviewing albums is the gems I find. I didn't remember that he was also a good producer. Most of the tracks he did are everyone's favorites below.

Treat Her Like a Prostitute/Slick Rick

The music sounds dated with the samples, beat and scratches, but Slick Rick's voice, demeanor and storytelling are so entertaining that you start to do the old school dances. Now for this to be the first song on the project is bold. It could turn off listeners or gain them by his entertaining bars. The title alone is degrading to women, but a good song is a good song.

The Ruler's Back/Jam Master Jay:

Let's shout out the legend JMJ first. Rest in paradise Jam Master Jay. This track sounds royal, and the Kingdom trumpets intro The Ruler as he slays the track. The Ruler has returned, and we are once again amazed by Slick Rick's vocal performance on the throne. And if you haven't bowed down to the Ruler yet, stop lying to yourself.

Children's Story/Slick Rick

I must tip my hat to Slick for creating entertaining music along with keeping my attention vocally. His storytelling ability is elite, great, and hilarious without being lame. This is one of those songs people know the rhymes too, but don't know who the artist is. Meaning the song is so popular that your grandmother, mother, and five-year-old sister know this joint. There are songs so popular people around the world can sing them word for word but forget the artist. The video is creative and fun and Slick Rick knocked them out the box on this one.

The Moment I Feared/The Bomb Squad

The track is calmer and more relaxing while Slick tells us a more serious story about some trials and tribulations that he feared. I hope this story isn't true at all. It does sound made up with drops of reality throughout.

Let's Get Crazy/The Bomb Squad

We get back into the funk of things with this up-tempo jazz track with the drums. Slick Rick is back in party mode and gets a bit crazy while his lyrics remain solid. Mr. Rick must be one of the most quotable rappers in our time.

Marquis Walker

Indian Girl (An Adult Story)/Slick Rick

This is one of my favorite stories Slick Rick has told throughout his career. His imagination and wordplay were just beyond his time. I'm pretty sure he was one of the first rappers that did voices on his own record. It's a record that you need to be mature enough to hear and appreciate. I'm pretty sure with the sensitive times now, the record is offensive in so many ways.

Teenage Love/The Bomb Squad

Another classic record that has Slick Rick in the conversation of originality. This record still has relevance with all teenagers and will always be. Teenage love is what many of us go through or are going through now. He needs to do a song called, "Adult Love ". The closest to my requested Adult Love story song is when Slick Rick rapped on De La Soul's Album, "AOI: Bionix" on the track, "What We Do (For Love)". Do y'all remember that joint? Rest In Paradise Dave from De La Soul.

I played Teenage Love thoroughly when I was a teen. Then I played it for my daughter when she was going through her teen years. This is a timeless record.

Mona Lisa/Slick Rick

Kiss the ring of this King. This song hits like the sun at its hottest temperatures. Mc Ricky D was brilliant with his verses, song structure and ability to keep you entertained. If you weren't rapping the verses, you were singing along to all the other lines of the record. The music still makes you dance, while the rap makes you get the hairbrush for your time to shine in the mirror.

Kit (What's The Scoop)/The Bomb Squad

The Black Knight Rider Rick rocked this joint. Being a fan of the original Knight Rider and how Slick Rick incorporated it in this rhyme was just so good. Mr. Rick was our rap lead field agent back then. The music still has me on my feet doing my famous two step dance routine.

Hey Young World/Slick Rick

Another hip-hop classic record speaking to the youth. And this song is still relevant, as Slick Rick schools us on being respectful and not getting into trouble. The message on this record lets me know that he cared for the youngsters. The music is solid, and the messages are appreciated to this day. It is hilarious how in one song he's spitting knowledge and the next he's telling you to lick the balls. A man of versatility.

Teacher, Teacher/The Bomb Squad

Throughout this album, Slick Rick has been a teacher, entertainer, and a poet doper than Halle Berry. Doper than her when she played a crackhead and doper than her real self. Halle Berry is the prettiest woman on

Marquis Walker

the planet and whenever I have a chance to speak on her, I do.

Again, Rick put in some work on this debut album and gave us his passion, drama, and braggadocious bars that put him on the rap Mount Rushmore in my book.

Lick the Balls/The Bomb Squad

This is a diss record to all his haters and he got them wondering if he was talking to them. The song shut down the project and had you flipping the tape cassette over for a relisten. Yes, I know we are in a digital age. I'm showing my age over here. The song is up-tempo to dance to, the DJ scratches were classic, and the rhymes were tough.

The album is incredible and still stands with other great albums in the genre of rap and to you who don't think so, Lick the Balls.

Chapter 6
READY TO DIE (SEPTEMBER 1994)

Biggie Smalls is the illest! He's one of the greatest rappers that has ever blessed the microphone. While he blessed this earth while rapping and spoke of various topics you may not have been comfortable with, he was still the KING of NY. Even as his flesh moves on, his spirit lives on.

When I first heard The Notorious BIG, it was a single he had brewing on the streets called "Party & Bullshit". I'm not sure if he was signed to Puffy yet. Or Diddy. Or Love. What is he calling himself these days? Anyhow, this song alone had me jumping out of my socks. His lyrical wordplay, delivery and idea for the song had me losing my marbles. Even the legendary 2PAC said he must have listened to this track 100 times when it was first released. I believe him; I must have listened to it 101 times. Rest in paradise Big and Pac.

Fact Checker News: Both the Notorious BIG and 2Pac's murder cases are still not solved.

He signed with Puff Daddy around 1992 or so. I remember B.I.G. saying so in a verse or an interview. Music back in the day took time to come out. So, people

Marquis Walker

had already been talking about this cat B.I.G. for a minute. The album BUZZ was in the air, but not in our ears, but it was worth the wait. On 9/13/94, our lives changed for the betterment of the genre.

Intro/Sean Combs

This intro is one of the longest to date. It gives you a glimpse of the artist's actual birth, his childhood, his street times, jail time, and the start of his rap career.

Things Done Changed/Darnell Scott

B.I.G. continues the story from the intro and gives us some low and highlights of his upbringing. His smooth delivery over this grimy and gangster track gives us a glimpse of what the album will sound like. When you listen to the majority of B.I.G., you're reminded that he was another quotable rapper who was taken from us too soon.

Gimme The Loot/Easy Mo Bee:

B.I.G.'s storytelling ability was one of the best since Slick Rick. I'm pretty sure he studied the best and became one of the best. I remember thinking there was a feature on this record, not knowing it was him the entire time. This record, he robbed everyone who had something he wanted while this beat rang out like his machine gun.

Cevere's Chronicles Vol. 2

Machine Gun Funk/Easy Mo Bee

The funk on this track is equivalent to your crusty socks balled up in the corner of your room, while The Notorious impressed us lyrically over and over. His flow is untouchable, and how he didn't write anything down still impresses me to this day. All rappers who have the talent to give me hip-hop goose bumps, I commend you. It's just a gift.

Warning/Easy Mo Bee

Easy Mo Bee was in his beat bag on this album and gave Biggie some highlights. The way Biggie put in layers of firearm verbal communication on these tracks had you literally ducking but listening with amazement. And have we talked about the skits yet? They matched the entire project throughout and were entertaining and funny at times.

Ready To Die/Easy Mo Bee

They say you can speak things into existence. This song gives me goose bumps because it's dope, but also because the artist is not here in the flesh. Was he ready to die? I'm pretty sure nobody is ready. Otherwise, the song is the title cut and plays its part as a great record.

One More Chance/Bluez Brothers & Chucky Thompson

This is the playboy record. B.I.G. was a P.I.M.P. even

Marquis Walker

though he didn't look the part. Most of the time, funny guys usually get the ladies, and he had humor and hustle which go a long way. Two things women respect and crave in a man are a good laugh and someone that works hard.

Once we realized the rapper had charisma, we just hoped he didn't have our women calling him Big Poppa. The producers turned these records with classic samples into classic songs to our generation as B.I.G. disrespected the women in his circle.

#!*@ Me/Sean Combs

Lil Kim and BIG got their acting chomps in on this skit. Or was it acting? We will never know unless Kim shares that information.

The What ft Method Man/Easy Mo Bee

This duet with another lyrical genius Method Man hits with force. The beat rings like the loudest bell as the MCs go back and forth with the best of them. It's another record that is unbelievable and you must stand up and give a standing ovation too. There were some members of Wu-Tang that didn't want this song to occur, but Method Man stood his ground and got the record completed. If y'all are not familiar, Ghostface Killah and Raekwon had minor beef with the Bad Boy camp for copying Nas's album cover. Back then, there was no copying allowed. Not even artwork or an album cover. The song is one of the best duets between rappers to this day though.

Juicy/Poke

This record is a top five record to this day from The Notorious. Of course, the producers used cheat codes with tracks that were already classic, but with Biggie's versus over them, they just added a cherry on top of your favorite sundaes. I'm pretty sure much of the world can quote this track in karaoke bars or in their showers.

Everyday Struggle/Bluez Brothers

The track slows down a bit while rapper B.I.G. tells you about his struggles to become an adult. The song is smooth, as B.I.G. tells how rough it was on his block. The way he told 3D stories took us to his block and at times would give us goose bumps. Not all rappers have this talent. It's like how some writers are more descriptive than others and it could make the story more exciting or boring. There is a middle ground and The Notorious had that gift to keep our attention, school us on various topics, and then still be entertaining.

Me & My B*tch/Bluez Brothers & Chucky Thompson

Many rappers did records similar, but they were referring to a gun as their B*tch. B.I.G. was referring to

Marquis Walker

his ride or die Bonnie as he took on the Clyde persona. The record speaks of love and how far you would go for it. It's a hip-hop Romeo and Juliet story to a certain extent.

Big Poppa/Chucky Thompson
The production was smooth and had Big Poppa flowing finer than a ballpoint pen. This song is the ultimate playboy/playgirl record. It's all about having a good time. Partying, eating well and hitting the skins. If you have or had women calling you Big Poppa, throw your hands in the air. Ladies put your hands in the air too if you got that good cootie cat making men do back flips and calling you Big Mamma.

Respect/Poke
This joint is harder than concrete under your feet. If you haven't earned respect for Biggie's flow by now, you may have to check your pulse. The reggae vibe and Biggie's verses made my famous two steps turn into four steps.

Friend of Mine/Easy Mo Bee
Biggie was correct to a certain extent on referring to chicken heads being foul. Yes, there are women out there who are scandalous, but we have a choice on who to allow in our circle. This is just a cycle of what went on

back in the days and still a bit today on ratchetness. Ladies and gentlemen, if you think like Biggie rapped on this record, you are not friends of mine.

Unbelievable/DJ Premier

The legend DJ Premier blessed the album with one track, but it is unbelievable. I wish he had more chances to create with the artist, but this track will have to do. The good news is he has more on his next album, which is just as good. And Biggie put this track in a headlock with his rap flow, causing us to want an entire project with the two. Big Poppa's voice box was an instrument as well, giving us magic on the mic and it was the illest.

Suicidal Thoughts/Lord Finesse

With the album called "Ready To Die", this song fits like the last puzzle piece. The song is dark as the night, but it relates to our thoughts. If you are having suicidal thoughts, please get help. Even though this was the last song, it was brilliant, big, and notorious.

The entire project is played in my household on more than one occasion every year. When I think of albums that I can play without the skip button, this is one of the first I think of. We were lucky and blessed to have Christopher Wallace's presents and his music is just a reminder that he was the King.

Chapter 7
REASONABLE DROUGHT (MARCH 2020)

The question is, who really is Stove God Cooks? Well, he was a student of rapper Busta Rhymes. He was a part of the Flipmode Squad at one time. Then Roc Marciano started to work with the young lad and this project was created. And I hope you're aware, when I'm writing I don't know these artists' every move, just what is public, so my stories will be short and brief. Now he's posting up with Westside Gunn and the Griselda Team in 2023. At the time of this project, though, he was under Mr. Marciano's wing, and they developed a project full of jewels that still shine to this moment.

If you've been following and been a fan of Roc Marciano, you should have heard Stove God Cooks a few times on Roc's album, "Marcielago". I became a fan of Stove God since hearing him there. And sometimes, all it takes is a feature or two to grab my attention for me to want to tap into that artist's work. Mr. Marciano warned us about this artist in a couple interviews that he blessed. Roc Marciano doesn't do much media, so when you can get him to talk it's a bonus.

I do recall Stove God Cooks featuring with the Flipmode Squad prior to working with Roc Marciano, but that's all I thought it was. We are now finding out that the artist was signed to Busta and Mr. Rhymes didn't know what to do with him. Either that or he was too busy with his career, Flipmode Squad, and then the sole careers of the Squad as well. But Busta was such a hot commodity back then, I'm pretty sure all acts were put on the sideline for his success. This was when Busta was in his prime.

I believe it was a blessing that Busta didn't have time, because things happen for a reason. And Reasonable Drought would have never happened.

On the first track, "Rolls Royce Break Lights", which is a great title for a song, Stove quotes, "God bless a homicide, God bless a shooter, your soul a computer, you google rumors." You already know this dude is trouble on the mic with verses like this. You will be quoting for days with lines like, "...left six pure, but I O.J. cut thirty" And this is just the premier track. This song alone will make you a fan of his.

Roc Marciano produced but didn't rap on this album. There are no features on the album, which gives more room to Stove God to show and improve.

Roc did bless us with the entire album's production though, which was more than enough. His beats take you to another world with the common head nod and the "StankFace" look. You know when you hear something, and your face resembles Conway the Machine. What's good, Conway? No disrespect Sir, just a way to

Marquis Walker

promote you when I can.

Stove God Cooks' lyrical ability is top notch. You will be sliding the bar back (rewinding) to hear what he said again and again. On Crosses he says, "...my daughter wearing chinchilla to the petting zoo." On "Break the Pyre" he says, "I do prayer while the Tesla drive itself, banging Mobb Deep, the bricks came whiter than Jon B." I can quote him all day, but that wouldn't be fair to my other reviews. This album is going to make other artists step their BARS up for sure.

And did I tell you this is his debut album? Y'all in trouble, rappers. And the fans of Stove God Cooks will benefit from all this Pyrex and coke talk because it's great wordplay, poetry at its best and entertainment.

In my book he comes second to Pusha-T when it comes to the continuous drug talk that stays interesting, fresh, and pure. It's like how Mobb Deep never got boring with street talk.

The team of Mr. Cooks and Mr. Marciano alone can compete with most collaborations of a rapper and producer. Most recently, at least in the underground scene, artists have been collaborating as such. Not everyone has that hip-hop magic like Snoop and Dre.

The highlight of this album is the blend of the tracks and above average lyrics. Smooth tempos and bars are consistent and fly like an eagle. On the "John $tark" song, Marciano's "1970s Uncle with plaid pants and but-

Cevere's Chronicles Vol. 2

terfly colla" wearing track goes beautifully with Stove's smooth lyrical dynamic. They have a fine-tuned relatedness throughout the entire project.

Stove God Cooks and Roc Marciano, if you're reading or watching my YouTube review, this album is reminiscent of any debut project from the greats.

I will continue to enjoy this and thank you for your beat selections, hard work, wordplay and thought process. I wonder if Jay-Z heard of this project. It's clever wordplay that will be broken down in universities hopefully. And for Roc Marciano, pass the marijuana you are smoking because your level of production is on another level. I don't break down each record because the album is a cohesive, brilliant work of art.

Chapter 8
THE ALLEGORY (FEBRUARY 2020)

This is one of those albums I was waiting for in 2020. This is the first five mic hip-hop album I thought was created in 2020. It wasn't the only one, but it started the year off just right. Now, if you haven't listened to this album yet, go in your room and put your BIG pants on and open your mind. This album is for ADULTS ONLY! And not because it's nasty, but because it's mature.

I'm calling this one of our hip-hop scriptures. From beginning to end, it's filled with gems about the world and how the artist sees it. If you have sensitive ears, don't listen to this album because you won't appreciate it. Royce murders every song on this album with strong opinions, truth, and daring delivery. His features stand on their own as well, like Benny the Butcher on "Upside Down", Kxng Crooked on "Tricked" and Westside Gunn on "Overcome"". And you know Conway the Machine did his thing on "FUBU". The entire Griselda got busy. Benny quotes, "We the Firm without Fox." There are more bars where that came from on this album than private prisons.

This project is musically soothing to the ears and soul. It's Royce's Chronic, Illmatic, Reasonable Doubt,

Cevere's Chronicles Vol. 2

College DropOut, 3 Feet High and Rising, DoggyStyle, The Fix, or whatever classic album you relate to. Look up these other albums if you've never heard of them, please. Do yourself a favor and tap in with my selections. If you don't agree with me, we can always have a hip-hop conversation.

All the production but one song was done by Royce. And like I said earlier, the music has brilliant melodies and it's melodic. It's an album you play from beginning to end. It's a project where you save the entire album on DSPs and cop the physical. Every time I listen to this album, it gets deeper with the lyrical awareness and Royce's direction of the content. It's like I catch something new with every listen.

Every track becomes a favorite depending on my mood, but they are all solid. I listened to this album over ten times when it was released and have lost count to now. Even though it's longer than the average albums being currently released, it has my interest throughout. Kind of like the Thriller album. HEE, HEE!

The highlights are the entire album. His lyrical content like on "Young World" is insane enough. He quotes, "...tell Trump don't send a Tweet, send a plumber to Flint." This dude is in his own world with bars right now. I won't spill all the bars; just go hit the play button after this. And then come back and let me have it with your opinions and thoughts. I'll be ready like Tiffany Haddish.

Marquis Walker

If you're reading this, Royce, tell us your daily regiments, so we can also use 100% of our brains. Seems like your entire cranium was lit on this album. And if you're really reading this, thank you. I'd like to thank you for this brave and incredible album. It's valiant because the content is positive, truthful, and educational. And you know people don't like to learn in their music, but you found a sweet spot that has me listening at the loudest volume and being intrigued as well. Thanks for the balance. I can't wait for your future production and lyrical content. This album is too long to break down each record, but every track does have something to offer. It comes a dime a dozen to put out great music with substance and Royce Da 5'9" is worth more than that dime.

Fact Checker News: Royce 5'9" is a rapper, producer and songwriter from Detroit, Michigan. His real name is Ryan Daniel Montgomery, and he's been active in the music industry since the 1990's. Worked with various artists, such as Eminem, DJ Premier, and Slaughterhouse.

This eighth solo studio album is thematically centered around the concept of allegory, which is a literary device in which characters and events represent abstract ideas or moral qualities. It delves into a variety of social and political issues, including police brutality, racism, and the prison industrial complex. The album has been praised for its ability to address complex issues in a nuanced and intelligent way, and for its contribution to the ongoing conversation about race and social justice.

Chapter 9:
Illmatic (April 1994)

This album is listened to and spoken about every year. If that doesn't make it a pure cut of cocaine and a classic, I don't know what does. People are always saying it's either Nas's best album or at least second. Now with Nas still creating, this album could be anywhere on someone's list. From the heavy, intricate sounds drowning the speakers to the even heavier lyrics coming out of Nas's mouth, we must bow down to this project no matter where it falls on your list.

This project is nothing less than perfect for me. And I know the word perfect should never be used, but there are certain albums that give you that vibe and this is one of them. Check for Marvin Gaye's "What's Going On" album or Prince's "Purple Rain" just to name a couple.

The highlights are that the entire album is a highlight. We all have an album from one of our favorite artists that we listen to at least once a year or more. Even with hip-hop putting out so much content, I still revert to this album at least three times a year. What are the albums you return to every year?

Let's continue, shall we? The producers include DJ Premier, Large Professor, L.E.S., Pete Rock, Faith N., Q-Tip and Nas. They put their best foot forward on this one and were just as hungry as Nas. Shoutout to the producers and the ones that made this project.

Did you know, Eric Sermon submitted C Type beats to this project that were never used? Mr. Sermon was so busy with all his artists, he was like, 'I'm not giving this dude he barely knew grade A beats.' I'm pretty sure he's still kicking himself in the butt cheeks for not being on this album. Another gem is that MC Search executive produced the album. Search for the group 3rd Bass and get the gas face while you step into the a.m. and kick 'em in the grill. Shoutout to MC Serch and his movement and determination to get Nas heard and get him a great production deal back then.

The intro has a clip of NAS on his first introduction song to the world. It was a song called, "Live at The Barbecue" by The Large Professor. Mr. Professor is a legendary producer who needs his own chapter. The intro record was a blend of where we first heard NAS. I'm guessing it was a real session back then and they just recorded it. They sound drunk and high for real.

Once the 2nd track drops with N.Y. State of Mind with those piano riffs and drums, you already knew this album was going to be special. His lyrical content pierces your soul, and you feel like you did when you first smoked marijuana. In the clouds and dizzy in a fun way. The album puts you in that zone. I'm pretty sure you can teach your kids with this album. It's very educational, entertaining, and thought-provoking.

The 3rd track is the only actual feature with the rapper killing a verse. Other features on the album are either the chorus or people talking. AZ blessed this track so insane that you would have thought it was his last verse before he got the death penalty. Even though I believe this is one of AZ's best verses ever, NAS still outshines AZ on this track. Sorry fans of AZ or AZ if you're reading. I'm just a huge Nas fan and hopefully I'm not coming off as biased. He's on my Rap Mount Rushmore without question. Nasty Nas is in the building.

I'm not going to review each track, but if I did, it would be done with the next sentence. Lyrically inspirational and educational with production with love, life, and reality. Check out some quotable verses that make you want to karaoke the entire album below. They should make a play or movie from this album. There is a book out though, that honors this album. Great read and is highly recommended. It's called, "Born to Use Mics: Reading Nas's Illmatic" by Sohail Daulatzai & Michael Eric Dyson.

"Halftime" - "I rap in front of more niccas than in the slave ship."

"It Ain't Hard to Tell" - "I drank Moet with Medusa, gave her shotguns in hell. From the spliff that I lift and inhale, it ain't hard to tell."

"One Love" - "Sometimes I sit back with a Budda

sack. Mine's in another world thinking how can we exist through the facts."

"Represent" - "Nas is a rebel of the street corner, pulling a Tec out the dresser. Police got me under pressure."

"Life's a Bitch" - "I switched my motto - instead of saying fuck tomorrow, that buck that bought a bottle could've struck the lotto."

Nas has more than one classical album and you will be hearing me speak on those in future readings. This album gives me hip-hop goose bumps every time I listen to it, and it takes me back to when I first heard it every time. From Nasty Nas to Nas to Essco or other names, he is one of the gods - period.

Chapter 10
LIVIN' LIKE HUSTLERS (FEBRUARY 1990)

We go west to Pomona, California, to visit K.M.G. & Cold 187um and the group Above the Law aka "ATL". This is their debut album, and back then the advanced promo cassette was released two months earlier. The producers were Above the Law, Dr. Dre and Laylaw. The executive producer is the late Eazy-E.

Murder Rap

The movie "Pineapple Express" featured this record in the movie. I love the samples of Public Enemy and Ice Cube aligned within the track. This was their first single. The song loops and samples give this track a vibe that you just vote for. The group had a great dynamic with the music and how they rapped was full of flavor.

Untouchable

This beat got me on my feet in the mirror acting out the entire song. It's one of those songs that you turn up when you're in the car to show off your speaker range. "New lyrics, breaking like a running rebel, for the words are defined, cause we're on a higher level." – K.M.G.

Livin' Like Hustlers

This track is so incredible and gives me a West Coast EPMD feel. They sampled "Comm 2" by the D.O.C. featuring Dr. Dre and MC Ren. The use of skits keeps you entertained and equips the music. The song screams out Pimp as it enters your soul. They had a great back and forth presence on the microphone. They were living like hustlers and rapping like Eric and Parrish. I still have this cassette tape.

Another Execution

This track makes you want to do crime for some reason. There are certain songs that can turn the party negative, and this is one of them. This is a classic song and hook from Dr. Dre and Cold 187um. "Why, Why, Why, It's just another execution!" The rappers had good storytelling abilities as well as flows.

Menace to Society

This song samples "Once you get it", by B.T. Express. Another group effort of the flow that we call Jada & Styles. The back-and-forth flow or back-to-back attack. When songs carry over four minutes and keep my attention, chalk it up to a good production and flow. With our attention spans shortening by the day, music as such should be praised and played. I believe I can rap this entire album. The project stands the test of time.

Marquis Walker

Just Kickin' Lyrics ft Dr. Dre

This record samples "More Peas" by Fred Wesley and J.B.s. The break and chorus drop elevates the song. The lyrics aren't always gangster; this track has a bit of humor. They slow it down with production but give you more to think about than a society full of menace. They just "kickin' lyrics".

Ballin'

This record samples "Why Have I Lost You" by Cameo. Again, the group does the EPMD back and forth technique and they seem to be at their best. We need to remember them when we start developing those lists about who's the best with the back-and-forth flow. The track is smooth and gives you that relaxing & cruising mood. Just drop the top of your ride and just coast at 2 miles an hour, so everyone sees you. Another player song that you tip your brim to as you tap your toes.

Freedom of Speech

"Now what's really known as a radio cut, when you can't say shit and can't say fuck." – Cold 187um & K.M.G. This is a good example of a revolutionary record. Even west coast gangsters had their fists high in the air like a pick comb. This is another song that highlights the project and brings substance along with a strong message. Cold 187 went in on this song, like he's seen some wild things in his upbringing.

Flow On (Move Me No Mountain) ft Dr. Dre

"They sayin', what's up, G's, tell me what's happening, I heard you're clockin' dollars, but you're still out here rappin'" – Cold 187um The music and rhymes were in tune with each other, making them classic. The production matched the group's vocals and made each record a hit. This is another smooth and playboy-type record giving you more respect for the duo.

The Last Song ft N.W.A.

This is a Posse cut that stands out and should be in the top 20 in hip-hop if we gather a list. This track's got you looking for a neck brace so you can continue to rock to it. This ruthless cut rings around the world, not just on the West Coast. These Niggas with Attitudes are entertaining, clever, humorous, and bar-worthy depending on who has the microphone.

Dr. Dre, MC Ren and Easy E without Ice Cube at the time were connecting with groups like Above the Law. This track gave ATL a boost since N.W.A. was already established in the industry. It's a very important album to the genre.

This record samples "Baby Let Me Take You (In Your Arms)" by Detroit Emeralds. "(We wanna fuck you Eazy) Yeah, you bitches scream, now bow down and praise

Marquis Walker

the lord for wing ding." – Eazy E Rip to the late rapper Eric Wright.

CHAPTER 11
THE SCORE (FEBRUARY 1996)

The 2nd and final album from the hip-hop trio the Fugees. Formerly named, "Tranzlator Crew", the Fugees won a Grammy Award in 1996 for "Best Rap Album." Their remake of "Killing Me Softly" won another Grammy Award for "Best R&B performance by a duo or group". This is one of those albums you present to people who have never listened to rap. It's a great introduction to the genre.

There are various producers, and they include Shawn King, Lauryn Hill, Wyclef Jean, John Forte, Diamond D and Handel Tucker. The bulk of the project was produced only by Lauryn Hill and Wyclef Jean.

Red Intro

Sounds like a preacher with a character incorporating the song titles in his speech to get us ready for the album.

How Many Mics

"Pick up your microphones. How many mics do we rip on a daily." – Fugees

Lauryn Hill's flow still stands the best of time. It's the 'what if' theory every time I hear her name or music.

Marquis Walker

The 'what if' she didn't take such a long break from hip-hop at the high point of her career. Wyclef musically controlled this track with the chorus, vibe, and tone of the record. Wyclef had character and charisma when he rapped. I always question Pras' stance in the group. He had a personality and seemed to be more of the jester of the group. He could rap, but his raps were not as memorable. And with his most recent situation in the news, let's pray for the brother.

Ready or Not

This is one of their biggest records to date. Classic even by itself. Some of Wyclef's best bars are on this record, it could be argued. He put his foot in the stew on this one. It's a verse that people repeat when it's on like they wrote it. Lauryn's controlling the chorus with her vocals and it's just beautiful. This also could be one of Lauryn's best lyrical performances as well. Very quotable. The chorus alone is a highlight. And as for Pras, he ripped this joint like old underwear.

Zealots

This record is underrated. It doesn't get its just due like others. The group's chemistry links like Raekwon's chain. Shoutout to Lauryn and Wyclef production and flow. They went against the laws of physics as Mrs. Hill stated within her rap. "And even after all my logic and theory, I add a "Motherfucker" so you ignant niggas hear me." – Lauryn Hill

On Wyclef's 2nd verse he brings up the fact that media were telling the guys of the group to retire and for Lauryn to go solo. I'm not sure if the press really got to this group, because that's exactly what happened. And let's not even get into Wyclef and Lauryn's relationship. I'm pretty sure that as that got rocky, so did the group's chemistry.

The Beast

This track sounds worldly, so let's praise Wyclef and Lauryn's production on this track and throughout the project. Lauryn highlights every track with MVP status. "Warn the town, the Beast is Loose." – Wyclef

The back and forth with Lauryn and Wyclef was the standout of the track as the music took us to other regions. Pras didn't rap until the three-minute mark.

This track has a bit of humor as well at the end, with the Chinese restaurant skit about BEEF. We are talking a double entendre of meat beef and the fight beef. The character said it best, you are "Just Bitch Ass Niggas!"

Fu-Gee-La

This is another record that just bleeds classic during play. Wyclef quotes, "We used to be number 10, now we're permanent at one, In the battle lost my finger, mic

Marquis Walker

became my arm." And with another great verse from Lauryn, she's on my Mount Rushmore of Hip-Hop for sure. And let's not forget Pras's verse in this song. He could rap and bring the heat at times; he was just overshadowed by Lauryn's powerful verses and Wyclef's personality on the mic.

Lauryn's balance of singing hooks and her out-rapping both her co-workers was just talent, passion, and greatness. The chorus is quotable and will have you thinking you can sing.

Family Business ft John Forte & Omega

This is a great posse cut. I wonder why Pras is not on it, but the song works otherwise. They took care of business on this record for sure.

When skits are mentioned, we must remember that The Fugees had some of the best. I like the skit at the end with Shannon Briggs, and how they transitioned for the next record with Lauryn's solo satisfactory record.

Killing Me Softly

The original was sung by Lori Lieberman but made more popular when Roberta Flack remade "Killing Me Softly with His Song", and Lauryn Hill made the record even more shiny and popular like Whitney did Dolly's record. This vocal performance took Lauryn to another level and platform immediately. This must be one of the most played records off this album. Such a beautiful rendition of the song. This record sampled "Bonita Applebum" by A Tribe Called Quest, making it one of the best R&B and rap records.

The Score ft Diamond D

This record stands out as well and includes production and a verse from the legend Diamond D. Diamond D quotes, "Come on son my stello's tight (uh-huh), 'cause by far, I'm the best producer on the mic (right?)" The song had me marching like I was a soldier or something. Songs like this are not only creative and hit the right head-nod patterns, but they make you miss the brigade's dynamic. The skit at the end is classic. It speaks on how men used to lie on their penis back in the day.

The Mask

Wyclef Jean quotes, "Have you ever worn the mask?" Are you camouflaging yourself people? This song is relevant to this day. I love the messages throughout this song and the album as well. The Fugees brought substance and value to the industry. Shoutout to the Fugees reuniting on stage in 2023 on stage. Will they do another album?

And Pras says, "(Well did you shoot him?) Nah, Kid, I didn't have the balls, that's when I realized I'm bumpin' too much Biggie Smalls." This is a standout verse for Pras.

Marquis Walker

Cowboys ft Outsidaz

This is the other Posse cut that stands out on this album. The pairing of both groups rapping together is brilliant. Wyclef and Pace Won traded verses. Then Lauryn Hill and Rah Digga traded verses. Then Pras and Young Zee joined in trading verses. John Forte went in by himself and added more Quotables. Is this one of the best Posse cuts in hip-hop?

The Outsidaz with The Fugees must be one of the best groups on group records to date. This record stood out like Alfalfa's hair. The skit at the end dealt with the tragic street tales of refugees of the hoods worldwide.

No Woman, No Cry

Wyclef's version of Bob Marley and the Wailers 1974, "No Woman, No Cry" was good. There are some classic records no artist should touch, but I must give Wyclef his props on this one. He did a stellar job. The song was written by Vincent Ford originally.

Manifest

Wyclef starts this joint off and adds energy to get you ramped up. I love the production from Hill and Jean. The samples and scratches stand out and scream hip-hop. Shoutout to the group Poor Righteous Teachers - if you love The Fugees, you will love Poor Righteous Teachers.

Pras took second place this time on this song when it comes to the bars. But again, Lauryn's verse stands out and manifests into your soul. The original album ends at thirteen tracks, but there are album versions with four other songs.

Chapter 12

Muddy Waters (December 1996)

This is Redman's 3rd album, and some people argue about his best work to date. The New Jersey Brick City Emcee has been in numerous barber shop conversations about him being a top five rapper depending on the year and album he dropped. He's always been on my Mount Rushmore of rappers.

Intro

This dream sequence of Jurassic Park gets the audience ready for an adventure of lyrics, stories, and just straight bars from Reggie Noble.

Iz He 4 Real/Eric Sermon & R. Noble

This is a short introduction with the rap Hall of Fame producer Eric Sermon on the boards and Reggie Noble aka Redman letting us know it's about to go down.

Rock Da Spot/E. Sermon & Tyrone Fyffe

Don't forget that E. Sermon was and still is one of the best producers. I'd like to know what strains of weed Redman was smoking when creating this project. His lyrical content, demeanor and flow were top notch.

Welcome (Interlude)/E. Sermon

This record is, "...Funkier than Haitian underarms!," Redman quotes. Even the interludes keep our necks snapping like a Slim Jim.

Case Closed ft Rockwilder & Napalm/Rockwilder

Not only did Rockwilder provide the hard sounds spilling out the speakers, but he also gave us the second verse. I learn something every day when I go back to tackling these great records. Shoutout to Napalm. All features solved the case.

Pick It Up/E. Sermon

The E-Double samples Zapp & Roger's "So Ruff So Tuff" from 1981. Redman turned it into a Weed Anthem record. Like Redman says, "If you find a bag of weed on the floor motherfucker, What the fuck you gon' do? Pick it up, pick it up." He also takes credit for the wild stuff like, "Listen, must we forget, I originated all that wild shit, that rrraahh rrraaoowww shit, that jump up and ready to fuck shit up now shit." Brick City baby!

N.I.N. (Skit)

It stands for Niggas in Newark. It's the neighborhood news reporter. Let's also remember that Redman had some of the best skits on his albums as well.

Marquis Walker

Smoke Buddah/E. Serman

This is another classic weed record that has a smooth and funky track that will have you doing your two-step dance with a blunt in your mouth and tissue in your nostril. The track makes you want to light one up and just sit back and relax. And if you're not smoking, get the funk out.

Fact Checker News: Shoutout to Tame One from the Artifacts rap group. Rest in paradise Tame. In an interview, Redman said Tame One taught him how to rap.

Whateva Man ft Eric Sermon/E. Sermon

This song will have you quoting Whateva Man all day. Let's give credit to Eric Sermon's rapping, producing, mixing, arranging and executive producing. He was a huge reason for this album being as great as it is. Redman's wordplay is so grimy and hood like that you forget his lyrics are top notch. This album created millions of pot heads.

Chicken Head Convention (Skit)

The hood rats aka chicken heads are represented at the Chicken Head Convention. I still know a couple of these ladies.

On Fire/E. Sermon

Eric is in his smooth, light one up bag of beats on this one, while Reggie adds more bars to his catalog. This track samples "Love and Happiness" by Al Green. The song is like Eric's saying, "Martini and Rossi, Asti Spumante", which are as smooth. We will be breaking down this album in hip-hop museums or universities soon. Don't get it twisted, Redman is still nice on the microphone.

Do What U Feel ft Method Man/Pras Michel

Pras from the Fugees blesses this track and gives it an Eric Sermon vibe. Red and Meth is one of the best duets as a rapping group and lyricist when they are on the same track. They challenge each other's pen game to the fullest. Go check out their group projects as they zone out on Blackouts.

The Stick Up (Skit)

Who else has skits this classic? Wu-Tang or Dr. Dre perhaps. Redman is always robbing people on these albums. This is not the only album Red robs people on either. It's a pattern.

Creepin'/R. Noble

Redman adds some production credits under his belt, putting this beat in the headlock. He produced his

Marquis Walker

second album "Dare Iz A Darkside" which got mixed reviews. There's no confusion about songs like this because he was creeping into hip-hop's top five after rapping like this. That's Jamal Phillips from the group, "Illegal" on the hook sampled.

It's Like That (My Big Brother) ft K-Solo/R. Noble & E. Sermon

Red and E team up on the production, while Redman's brother from the Hit Squad K-Solo joins the party on the microphone. Their back-and-forth bars are definitely a highlight on this project, even though Mr. Solo's voice sounds like he swallowed the weed instead of smoked it. Dope record.

Da Bump/E. Sermon

This record samples Rick James' joint "Bustin' Out". Erick Sermon is one of the best producers on the planet. Your props are given E-Double. The way he orchestrated entire albums in the past to now; his work ethic is remarkable. And he brought out the best in Redman and his lyrical aggressive flow.

Uncle Quilly (Skit)

Redman did many voices, and this is one of his best. Uncle Quilly is at the Freak-Neck in 1996 talking trash to some chicken heads. Very hilarious.

Yesh Yesh Ya'll/E. Sermon

This track samples Common's "I Used to Love H.E.R." and Dr. Dre's "Nuthin' But A 'G' Thang" freestyle remix. And who was funking with Redman back then? He quotes, "It's a thin line between love and hate, it's a thin line between the trigger and the finger of a .38." Just more bars than an American prison.

What U Lookin' 4/R. Noble & Rockwilder

This song hits the political front and questions the police's bad practices. It's another record with a smooth flow but it adds substance and a wake-up call to the streets. It's Redman's "F", the police record.

Soopaman Luva 3 Interview

In 1990, N.W.A. spoke about not biting the johnson. Did Jane not get the memo? Soopaman Luva got the reporter slobbing the knob, but her teeth got in the way.

Soopaman Luva 3/E. Sermon & Redman

Redman continues his story about his superhero who is more hood than abandoned brick buildings. He starts the song off with a smooth track and flow and then gets funkier. It's a two-for-one track with Soopaman clowning Parrish Smith after EPMD broke up. This record is clever, entertaining, and funny.

Marquis Walker

Rollin'/E. Sermon

This head nodding track sampled "Microphone Fiend" by legendary group Eric B. & Rakim, and Curtis Mayfield's "(Don't Worry) If There's A Hell Below, We're All Going to go". And as you're rolling another get-high stick, Redman is rolling over this funky beat with his dirty boots. "F" your couch.

Da Ill Out ft Jamal & Keith Murray/E. Sermon

Hope it's not too soon, but Red says, "Get you hollerin', like Marvin Gaye, when his father shot him in the chest, I roll with two stacks of tecs." This is the typical posse cut those rappers added to the end of their projects. And this track was on some hardcore stuff with Keith and Jamal. They ripped this track to pieces - especially Jamal aka Mally G. The album started hard and ended hard. Shoutout to long albums that remain quotable, entertaining, and bring you to your feet. And Redman, if you ever put out the 2nd installment of this album, wake me up. I'm still waiting for Muddy Waters 2.

CHAPTER 13
REASONABLE DOUBT (JUNE 1996)

I remember Nas's "It Was Written" coming out around the same time as this. I believe Nas's came out a week later. I went downtown Boston with some friends to the record store to purchase this album. If I'm not mistaken, the album drops back then were on Tuesdays. I played this album so much that week that I almost forgot to go grab the Nas joint.

When I eventually purchased, "It Was Written," I finally put this album down. Since Nas put out "Illmatic" the world of hip-hop and me were more excited than a kid going to Disney. Now, was Nas's 2nd album good? Of course, it was. Some people to this day say it's better than Illmatic.

What I do remember myself doing though was listening to Jay-Z's debut Reasonable Doubt more that summer and beyond. To this day, I pick Reasonable Doubt over It Was Written. And I'm a bigger Nas fan than Nas's reflection.

Can't Knock the Hustle ft Mary J. Blige/Knoboy, Dahoud Darien & Sean C

This record starts off with a brief introduction with top notch singing from Queen Mary, great production,

Marquis Walker

and top tier lyrics from Jay. With Mary on top of her R&B game and Jay-Z being in his "Optimus Prime" of rap, the song just made sense. Jay-Z said, "My pops knew exactly what he did when he made me; tried to get a nut and got a nut and what!?"

Politics as Usual/Ski

This track is smooth and bangs on different levels while Jay continues to submit rewindable clear, clever, and street politics that are quotable. I remember just rewinding this cassette tape on numerous occasions, saying who is this dude?

Brooklyn's Finest ft The Notorious BIG/Clark Kent & Dame Dash

This record must be top five duet rap songs period. The way the top emcees at that time blazed the microphone with the back-and-forth flow, was remarkable and still stands the test of time. Rest in Paradise to Biggie. This is a record that people still speak about, and which is played continuously. They are still Brooklyn's finest.

Dead Presidents 2/Ski Beatz

Every time I hear this record, I think of the Jay and Nas beef that started because Nas never gave Jay-Z a feature in the beginning of Jay's career. On "Takeover"

Jay says, "So yeah I sampled your voice, you was using it wrong, you made it a hot line, I made it a hot song." This record's production was fire and gave me a euphoric feeling. Jay says, "I dabble in crazy weight without rap, I was crazy straight, partner, I'm spendin' money from '88, what?" Jay burned this track with Nas on the hook.

Fact Checker News: For your information, Nas owns a portion of this record. So even though Nas signed with Jay later after their feud, Nas owns something of Jay's and Jay doesn't own music from Nas.

Feelin' It ft Mecca/Ski Beatz

This classy jazzy lounge tune gives you the impression that Jay is at a smokey club on one of those old fashion mics. The beautiful voice from Mecca made me feel this record. Jay says, "I feel my mind sometimes I hear myself moaning, take one more toke and I leave that weed alone, man."

D'evils/DJ Premier

Premo is responsible for more classic records and albums than whoever you can spit at me. With a Snoop and Mobb sample with his lovable scratches, DJ Premier embodied this joint. Type hip-hop on Google and Premo's face should pop up. Jay-Z matched the track

Marquis Walker

with incredible bars like, "She said the taste of dollars was shitty, so I fed her fifties, about his whereabouts I wasn't convinced, I kept feedin' her money 'til her shit started to make sense." Some people wonder if this is a shot at 50 Cent.

22 Two's/Ski Beatz

We back in the elite Black lounge with Jay entertaining the crowd with a freestyle on twenty-two twos. It's clever and Jay can kick it like the legends A Tribe Called Quest. Shawn Carter aka Jay-Z doesn't use a pen, so all his rhymes are freestyle pretty much. He's a brilliant emcee who is already on my Mount Rushmore of Hip-Hop with his alien-like lyrics. I loved Maria Davis in the introduction and checking the dude smoking weed at the end.

Can I Live/DJ Irv Gotti

Irv samples "The Look of Love" by Isaac Hayes while Jay-Z speaks about the drug game and dropping jewels on the way. The song is about having a good work ethic at the end of the day. The jazz record gives me a melodic feeling and his rapping ability will always be discussed in lyrical conversations as long as we live.

Ain't No Nigga ft Foxy Brown/Jaz-O

Jay-Z's brother from another mother produced this

track and sampled The Four Tops' "Ain't No Woman (Like the One I've Got)" on the album's second single off the project. With Foxy Brown in her status at the time, this made the record another top duet record. They were like lightning and thunder on this song, both providing sparks that highlighted their careers. Jay's verse was sick, but Foxy's was coronavirus sick. This was the first time I heard Ms. Brown on a record, and I became a fan of hers, just off this verse alone.

Friend or Foe/DJ Premier

This was a quick headbanger that had Jay checking his enemies really quick in less than two minutes. Mr. Z shuts it down with, "Don't ever, ever, ever come around here, no more," to his foes.

Coming of Age ft Memphis Bleek/Clark Kent

Clark Kent put his production stamp on this fire song. This is the third good duet record from Jay. This time his other brother from another, Memphis, joins the party. These must be some of Bleek's most memorable bars to date. Jay-Z was passing the torch and teaching the youngster the game.

Cashmere Thoughts/Clark Kent

That's Clark Kent and Jay going back and forth with the pimp talk. This song was supposed to only have one

Marquis Walker

verse, but Mr. Kent convinced Jay to do a second and add the song to the album. The first verse made the Source magazine in their Hip-Hop Quotable section.

Bring It On ft Jaz O & Sauce Money/DJ Premier

This is the record that Nas and AZ were supposed to be on. I'm pretty sure it's the reason Jay brought the beef on. Since they were a no-show, they incorporated Big Jaz and Sauce Money. The song came out good anyway because all rappers on the record wanted the best verse. It made the record stand out lyrically off this DJ Premo astonishing track with the Fat Joe sample.

Regrets/Peter Panic

This laid-back track took Jay on a vibe to be vulnerable and speak on gangster survival. The beat reminds me of sunshine, good times, and hope without regrets. As Jay says, though, "In order to survive, gotta learn to live with regrets."

Like I mentioned prior, this album had me in a fog. It's one of those albums that you listen to at least once a year. I listen to it more than that. Thanks Damon Dash, Shawn Carter, and Kareem Burke of Roc-A-Fella Records.

Chapter 14

ONLY BUILT 4 CUBAN LINX... (AUGUST 1995)

This is an album that is connected to color. Call it the "Purple Tape" and the real hip-hop heads will know exactly what you're referring to. Producer RZA was so in his prime of producing, executive producing and keeping the peace with nine or more members that he should get an award just for that.

This album was the third solo album from the Wu-Tang members. First it was Method Man, then Ol' Dirty Bastard, and then what we now call the Purple Tape, Only Built 4 Cuban Linx.

Striving for Perfection/RZA

This was an intro that set up the album and continued the Wu Dynasty. It was like the hood mafia cinematic beginning of a movie. They are putting their plans on the table and talking about growing.

Knuckleheadz ft Ghostface Killah & U-God/RZA

This is a money record that smacks fire out of you. The RZA's production is so original and authentic that when people tried to duplicate it, they failed. Rae was speaking on the Clan and their daily tales, while Ghost robbed people on his verse. U-God put in a tough verse too.

Marquis Walker

I always wondered why they never put out a Wu-Tang slang dictionary. We will need one when this album is in the hip-hop museum or studied in universities.

Knowledge God/RZA

This track takes me on a cloud or somewhere godly, while Rae throws darts about prison and getting that dollar, dollar bill yawl. The chorus alone is quotable and rewindable. Rae's voice and flow made him one of the hottest rappers back then.

Criminology ft Ghostface/RZA

This was the 2nd single released off the project. RZA's production is stellar and just fantastic, and still holds up today with those Scarface samples. Ghost laced them on this track while Rae brought the pain with bars like, "Yo, fuck that, criminology rap, sneakers stay jet black floatin' n the flyest Ac' nigga."

Incarcerated Scarfaces/RZA

RZA's passion for hip-hop was 400% during this era and this could be Rae's best solo record or at least top five. This record is totally quotable, and his delivery was top notch. This is that song that will have you do a two-step dance and get the hairbrush for a mic in the mirror.

Rainy Dayz ft Ghostface Killah & Blue Raspberry/RZA

This track is one of RZA's favorite Wu-Tang tracks he produced; he said in an interview. It's a beautiful record. Blue Raspberry sings like a bird and sings for Rae, but he isn't here. Rae & Ghost are spitting on getting out of poverty and this could easily be a six-mic song.

Guillotine (Swordz) ft Ghostface Killah, Inspectah Deck & GZA/RZA

Did anyone check on RZA's temperature back then, because he was a production phenomenon. This track brought Wu back and all members sharpened each other's swords. The violin sample track had the members on another level of rap. Shoutout to GZA for shutting down the track as the head of Voltron.

Can It Be All So Simple (Remix) ft Ghostface Killah/RZA

Their skits were classic too. The intro to this record is so good it makes you want to slap someone up too. It's the reality of survival in the hood and it's not that simple. The original track is on the 36 Chambers Enter the Wu-Tang album. Shoutout to the chorus from Rae and Ghost, "Dedicated to projects with Black kids. Dedicated to man who built pyramids."

Shark Niggas ft Ghostface Killah (Biters)/RZA

This skit is famous in hip-hop. It sparked off some

Marquis Walker

beef when The Notorious B.I.G. bit off Nas album cover. Back in the day, there was no duplication of rap sound or artwork. People were original. Today's rap uses an algorithm and shoots out rappers like a factory of G.I. Joe collectables.

Ice Water ft Ghostface Killah & Cappadonna/RZA

This is the first track Cappadonna blessed after being released from jail. U-God summoned him to the studio, and he laced this airy dope track. Ghost & Rae stamped the package as usual. I always thought Ghost and Cappa should have done an album back then.

Glaciers of Ice ft Ghostface Killah, 60 Second Assassin & Masta Killa/RZA

Another great skit intro to the record about wallabies' shoes as RZA added another incredible track to his catalog. Masta Killa put a dent into this track while Rae and Ghost continue to impress with lyrical wordplay. The most important bars were from Ghost, "My seeds grow with his seeds, marry his seeds. That's how we keep Wu-Tang money all up in the family." Ghost was speaking on family wealth back then.

Verbal Intercourse ft Nas & Ghostface Killah/RZA

Nas sparks this classic record to the womb to the tomb and represents. Ghost & Rae matches Nas's lyrical performance and makes this record rewindable. This song is a double five mic. It's the best product on the block.

Wisdom Body ft Ghostface Killah/RZA

This is a solo track for Ghostface Killa. Raekwon had a verse, but RZA took it off based on how personal the song was for Ghost. I remember listening to this song and not noticing Rae was missing at one point. The brothers Rae and Ghost work so well together that sometimes they sound alike. And this was their album, even though it says Raekwon on the cover. It's just like Ghostface Killah's album "Ironman" where Rae was all over too.

Spot Rusherz/RZA

There's a St. Ides commercial in the background while the members talk about feeling someone may be hit that day. We all have a feeling that something bad could happen at times. Reakwon's storytelling is underrated. This record about a drug dealer stick-up kid who plots and robs a hood intruder was good.

Ice Cream ft Method Man, Ghostface Killah & Cappadonna/RZA

Cappadonna says, "I love you like I love my dick size." Shoutout to Cappa and his underrated verses back

Marquis Walker

in the day. The entire team added their flavors of cream to this record. This song and video would get twenty microphones if the Source Magazine was still relevant. This could be a top five posse cut in hip-hop, period. It's another anthem record for Wu-Tang Clan.

Wu-Gambinos ft RZA, Ghostface Killah, Method Man & Masta Killa/RZA

Who didn't enjoy the skits that introduced songs as such? Method Man opened this song and made others step their pen game up. I go back and forth on who I am in the mirror rapping for my private talent show. Props to the Wu-Gambinos.

Heaven & Hell ft Blue Raspberry & Ghostface Killah/RZA

Love this track and the song's message. Rea & Ghost should have done more albums together. This song and album got me craving their voices together going back and forth with fluidity, value, and just dope music. They say, "What do you believe in, heaven or hell? You don't believe in heaven 'cause we're living in hell." So poetic.

North Star (Jewels) ft Popa Wu/RZA

RZA sampled Barry White's "Mellow Mood" on this record. Popa Wu is on his pulpit giving jewels and sounding pimpish. To sum up the entire album, Method said it best, "Wu roll together as one, I call my son' (sun) 'cause he shine like one." Wu-Tang forever!

Chapter 15

ACT LIKE YOU KNOW (SEPTEMBER 1991)

I've been a fan of MC Lyte since she branched onto the scene of hip-hop. Her voice is the most distinctive, lovely, and sexy instrument that I'm aware of. I've never met her, but she would be someone I would fan out to. It's good to hear her doing voice overs for cartoons, award shows and more with those vocals.

Album "Act Like You Know" is the fourth studio album from MC Lyte. This is when her albums matured a bit, incorporating more funk and soul elements. Here's my breakdown of the tracks on the album:

When in Love/Wolf & Epic

This is a great rap love record that could be in anyone's top five list. The music is orchestrated very well along with the background vocals. It's a dance record as well, not just a song that teaches you about love. It's like let's Cha Cha Slide and do the Kid 'n Play while we fall in love.

This song and album have MC Lyte rapping at a high tier. And when in love, people are not themselves. I agree with her one hundred percent.

Eyes Are the Soul/Epic & Wolf

Loving the jazz tempo and vibe. MC Lyte's storytelling is underrated. She balances subject matter, relationships, and positive messages, while making you want to dance and learn the lyrics.

It's an upbeat track with a catchy hook and talks about the importance of inner beauty.

Search 4 the Lyte/King of Chill

The artist flips the subject of light in various ways, including her name of course. The song is clever, with heavy drums leading the way. Loving the DJ scratches and the mix of the record. Her life messages give you hope and light at the end of the tunnel.

Act Like You Know/Wolf & Epic

The title track is one of my favorites. The beat is still relevant and gives you the head nod factor while Lyte speaks highly of herself. Y'all better act like you know. I knew, once I heard this beautiful woman back in the 80s, that she would be influential for the culture.

Mickey Slipper (Interlude)/Epic & Wolf

Even the interludes with the rapper were entertaining and made you want it to be an entire song. This is Lyte's public announcement on going out and drinking.

Marquis Walker

Poor Georgie/Dee Jay Doc

Another record that MC Lyte put in a headlock with this amazing track. It's another story record that teaches a lesson but is entertaining as well. There's another dope public announcement sponsored by Lyte Entertainment about drinking and driving, which flowed well off the interlude Mickey Slipper. The chorus is very quotable, while the MC gives a speech on loving the people while they are here, so you won't regret it later.

Take It Off/Pal Joey 2

Lyte is asking for the draws on this record. She's not ashamed of herself on this record. You must go after what you want and be aggressive ladies at times. Ladies, go to the Lyte and ask for the 3rd leg and tell your mate to take it off.

The DJ went off on this record with his scratching performance. He put on a show. The record is a bit bold and aggressive, but what male artist hasn't crossed that line? Now these types of records are above and beyond, and the women artists aren't asking politely, they are more descriptive on getting to the penis.

Beyond the Hype/Epic & Wolf

This record sounds like a rap & rock record and gives me an anthem vibe. Shoutout to Bill Trudel for tapping in the background and singing with great energy and passion. The music and instruments immediately keep me hyped and give me positive vibes. This record and album are inspirational. This would be a great album to let your children hear. I'd advise having an open dialog as well.

All That/Audio Two

This record samples "This Song is Familiar" by Funkadelic and starts off like it's about to be a church record. Then MC Lyte adds some grit and personality. The rapper puts her foot in this dude's butt cheeks as he tries to be fast on the date. Sounds like Lyte knows her worth, and she is not having that. It also sounds like she's got the razor under the tongue just in case.

Big Bad Sister/45 King

The legendary 45 King blesses this track while the artist reps many places she rocks with. This track has the formula of hip-hop with a dope beat, great lyrics, smooth scratches, and it makes you want to breakdance. It seemed like MC Lyte didn't curse much but cursed only when the record needed it.

Like That Anna/Audio Two

This is like another quick interlude and Lyte wasted no time smacking other MCs with less than a minute of freestyling. Rappers used to quote and repeat, "It's like

Marquis Walker

that anna" when they freestyled in cyphers.

Kamikaze/45 King

It seems like the last couple of songs, Lyte is talking that fiery rap. She says, "All you rappers, you fucking impersonators, saying I'll rap now and learn how to rap later." She went kamikaze on this joint spitting at these wack rappers. This song is still relevant. Lyte was a Rough Neck at times too.

Can you Dig It/King of Chill

MC Lyte always had the "IT" factor when it came to music. Some of the track's sound like they belong to the 90s, but they still rock. I can dig it like how she's smacking these corny rappers literally on these records.

Like a Virgin/45 King

Mr. King is back with another banging track while rapper tackles the track like a defensive end. Lyte is a great storyteller and very entertaining while she teaches us lessons. She keeps your attention like Madonna and teaches little homie how to do the nasty even though it was her first time. This is another song that was bold for the 90s and Lyte broke many barriers in the music business.

Lola from the Copa/Audio Two

Let's give Audio Two some credit for giving Lyte some classic tunes, including this one. It's another beautiful story from MC Lyte about love, sex, lust, romance and the ups and downs of Lola. She speaks on rape culture and warns the listeners on the downsides of life. Then the story takes a right turn with a twist and Zeek the Freak caught a bad one. Wrap up kids.

2 Young 4 What/DJ Master Tee

This record samples "Groove with You" by Isley Brothers. Lyte's trying to get her groove back with a younger man and he's not with her flirting and passes. The lyrics are a bit controversial by today's standards. The second and third verse sound a bit rapist-like depending on when she wrote this record. I'm surprised the record company didn't take this song off.

Absolutely Positively…Practical Jokes/45 King

Love this story as well. Where does MC Lyte fall when it comes to storytelling rap? She is good. This is a song about karma. She played jokes on her neighbor and the neighbor got a bit of revenge.

Marquis Walker

Another Dope Intro/Epic & Wolf

The last quick interlude rap that MC Lyte went in hardcore. She lets you know she's that rapper not to be messed with.

K-Rocks the Man/Audio Two

Not sure why they added this record to the party, but K-Rocks' down with Lyte's movement, so I'm guessing it was because he was going to drop an album next. Rappers used to do this with group members. Wu-Tang was the best at it. Even though this is a skippable record for me, it doesn't have Lyte on it, so I don't count it.

All and all these records are great. The album has positive messages, great storytelling, dope bars and the music makes you want to dance. What else do you want from an album? You better Act Like You Know.

Chapter 16

LAST CHANCE, NO BREAKS (OCTOBER 1995)

Prior to this album, this young gentleman at the time was in a group called "Illegal". And prior to that, he was running the streets and getting in trouble and upsetting his grandmother. His history is explained in track two, "Keep It Live", if you want to connect the dots. The dots I want to connect are, great producers and a great emcee equal a great album.

The stars were aligned for this artist and from the beats, features, and rapping, you must appreciate this work of art. So, when you think of Philadelphia, think Jamal.

Live Illegal/Easy Mo Bee

Does Easy Mo Bee have a psychic ability to connect himself with great projects? He's always in the mix when it comes to songs that bring heat to hip-hop. Easy Mo is a genius when on the boards and wheels of steel. Jamal aka Mally G was in rare form on this song and entire album.

Keep It Live/PME

This is another solid track that got Jamal in a good rhythm to add true value to his discography. Jamal is in

Marquis Walker

story mode speaking on "Back in the Day" bars. His history deals with crime, family, and this rap industry. Well, at least those are the highlights he talks about. His flow is genuine and superb and entertaining on high levels.

Situation/Erick Sermon & Rockwilder

Again, Jamal has a knack for storytelling and entertaining us on the microphone. I can quote this entire song and act it out in the mirror. The track is tougher than burnt steak and the lyrics will give you appreciation for the culture of hip-hop.

Insane Creation ft Redman/Easy Mo Bee

Easy Mo Bee is back on the track giving Mally G a grimy and head-nodding sound. With Redman trading verses back and forth with Jamal, it made his pen sharper. This song is hotter than bad breath. The record is rewindable and makes you want to go back to listen to Redman's classic albums.

Jamal went toe to toe with Funk Doc the Spot, Redman. Give Easy Mo Bee and Redman their props because they elevated this song to the fullest. As a matter of fact, start sending all artists and people you love gratitude while they are here with you.

Fades Em All/Redman & Rockwilder

Do you hear what is coming out of your speakers?

This song is hotter than the Earth's core. Shoutout to the production from Redman and Rockwilder. The music is hyper, funky, and gives you a stank face. There's a Pete Rock version of this record in rotation also. Jamal says, "Now who the fuck want to see Jamal, I fades them all!" If you don't believe he was one of the best rappers in the '90s, I need you to get a hearing aid.

The Game/Redman

Redman is a great producer. He's known for his raps but let's remember he can get busy behind the boards too. The production is stellar, dark, and dank. Just as funky as Redman's socks. Again, Jamal controls the microphone throughout the record with his storytelling abilities. People slept on this album. The artist spit more game on this song than Lebron in the finals.

Da Come Up/Mike Dean

It's producer Mike Dean's turn to turn up the party a bit. This beat is colder than your ex dumping you for someone uglier on Valentine's Day. If y'all don't get the "F" up and bow down to this track, please submit your hip-hop card. The skit blended well with the West Coast track, giving Jamal a platform to float on like a cloud. Jamal really put his pen game to work. The content is a bit rough for the ears, but the lyrics are just as good as any of your favorite rappers.

Marquis Walker

Don't Trust No/Mike Dean

I'm going to put it in the shortest terms known to man. This song and album rocks like rock n roll and hip-hop had a baby. The track is so funky, George Clinton tried to smoke it. The record's got you screaming and quoting Mally G, "Don't Trust No, B!tch!" This track stands out over other songs, even though every song on the project is a standout. This song is like Beyonce in the group Destiny's Child. Kelly and Michelle could sing, and they are just as beautiful, but we all know who the star is.

Keep It Real/Erick Sermon

Erick Sermon with this piano-heavy, smooth track got me bobbing my head like a bobblehead.

The song is stylish, relaxing, graceful, tasteful, and refined like fine wine. Erick Sermon is my hero on the production side. I thought he'd produced this entire album when I first heard it, but I'm sure he gave the final say on the production. He's a legend, period. And Jamal put it down on this song. He kept it real tight with his wordplay and had me rewinding this song like 12 times when I first heard it.

Genetic for Terror ft Keith Murray, L.O.D., Redman & Erick Sermon/Redman & Rockwilder

What is a 90s album without a posse cut? This track

bangs like a horny teenage boy who just discovered sex. Keith Murray and his group L.O.D. were problems back then. This song reminds me that lyrics matter.

It's a good posse cut and stands the best of time, because it still rocks like a basehead dancing for a discounted rock. I listen to this album at least once a year. I will never forget to bump this entire project. Def Squad was an issue like police locking up Black people. They cared about hip-hop, and their passion showed on the microphone.

Unf**kwittable ft George Clinton & Passion/Erotic D

They could have ended the project with the outstanding posse cut, but if you have a chance to work with George Clinton, this should be the intro and outro. Producer Erotic D must have sniffed Mr. Clinton's boots before lacing this track. It's funky! Funkier than a track marathon runner after running a long race in 100-degree weather.

Rapper Passion put in work on this song. She stamped this package like it was going international. Passion stomped this beat with wheat classic Timberlands. Jamal let her rock and it paid off. This is one of my favorite cuts on the album. And then, when Passion was done, Jamal reminded the world that this was his project and put his pen game to work. I wonder what happened to Passion. She was a good rapper. This album

Marquis Walker

gives me hip-hop goose bumps and reminds me that the 90s was one of the best decades of the genre.

Chapter 17
JEWELZ (AUGUST 1997)

If you look up underrated emcees in the game, O.C. would be smiling in a photo like the Kool Aid man. He's just one of the best rappers and he could go toe to toe with some of the best. If you mention his name in the industry, I'm pretty sure this project would come up. Let me break it down for you. Ah, one two, Ah one two.

Intro/Patrick Moxey & Dave Supter

This was just a brief jazz funk instrumental.

My World/DJ Premier

This is one of the best hip-hop songs in history. DJ Premier was in his beat bag like no other. Every time I hear DJ Premo beat, my heart beats double time. O.C. says, "It's my world and I won't stop and if you stand in my way, you're bound to get dropped." This sums up the song alone. Let's give O.C. his props now before I go on.

War Games ft Organized Konfusion/DJ Premiere

Another classic Premo joint to date and features Organized blessing the mic with O.C. Prince Po and Pharoahe Monch went back and forth briefly and added some value, and O.C. went in on this song like he was going to war with other rappers.

Can't Go Wrong/Ogee

This song has a smooth jazz feel with a great singalong chorus, "You got me hypnotized, mesmerized." O.C. is getting his love poetry on to a special someone. This is the song you play for your lady for appreciation. It has a groove to it that can even be played at a wedding.

The Chosen One/Buckwild

The track starts off with a different beat that gets your toes tapping and then spins off to smooth jazz track to relax your soul. I'd enjoy sitting down speaking with this artist and getting his story behind this entire project and just his life experiences. The words he speaks give you energy, love, entertainment, skill, and poetic gifts.

Dangerous ft Big L/Da Beatminerz

This song comes on and slams in your ears like Onyx. Da Beatminerz gave O.C. a highlight record that could be a club and street record. With Big L on this record, we get pure cocaine like bars. Bars that are sharper than those knife commercials that come on at 2 AM. Big L was feared on the microphone back then. And the way O.C. and Big L went back and forth. It's some of the best I've heard from a duo that went back-to-back. Rest in Paradise Big L. He was one of the best to ever grip a microphone and pour his heart into this world. This song is rewindable, quotable, and makes you want to blast it at the highest levels. Big L says, "I know you want me, hoe, if I was you, I'd want me too, Bitch." Again, rest in Paradise Big L. You died too soon.

Win the G ft Bumpy Knuckles/DJ Premier

The skit prior to the track is just as classic as the record. It sets up the battle between whatever suckers are going to lose to Bumpy and O.C. Bumpy Knuckles aka Freddie Fox features are always classic with bars to rewind and say, "Oh my" too. They both crushed this beat and won that prize of a thousand dollars with ease.

Far from Yours ft Yvette Michele/Buckwild

Again, the track starts off with a separate beat and then transitions into a smoothed-out track to ride to. O.C. puts in that bar work, as singer Michele balances the track with a sensual songbird chorus. This track is above average, so don't bite his style because it's far from yours.

Marquis Walker

Stronjay/Da Beatminerz

The dark, grimy and hype track gives O.C. a platform to throw some strong lines to the lady in his eyesight. Beautiful women will have you rapping this smooth with charisma. This shows that the artist can tell some of the greatest stories in the booth. Creating a hip-hop love story is a gift, and the artist tagged this Beatminerz track like a NYC train in the 80s.

M.U.G. ft Freddie Fox/DJ Premier

Freddie joins O.C. again, this time on a classic Premo beat that's hilly like rocks in the mountains. Feature Mr. Fox always has memorable verses when he stamps anyone's record. And what would hip-hop be without a DJ Premier scratch? I'd pay millions if I had them, just for a DJ Premier scratch. And whenever rappers go back-to-back on a song as good as these rappers, I'm tapped in like a teenager on social media.

The Crew/Showbiz

The producer from the group Showbiz & AG joins the party and gives O.C. a dark and dank banging track. This allows O.C. to tell a story that is interesting and entertaining. O.C. says, "His demeanor wasn't pure, I know this for sure, he had a diseased look that the world couldn't cure." I always wondered why O.C. never got the same attention in hip-hop as Nas. He's just as worthy.

You and Yours/Ogee

These days songs were longer than some of these rappers' entire albums. You must have a good attention span to appreciate music as such. The music rocked and the rhymes were intriguing and glorious. O.C. says, "To get a response, control shit at the snap of a finger like I'm the Fonz." The 90s were full of Happy Days.

Hypocrite/Buckwild

Legendary producer Buckwild sampled "Sensitize" by Roy Ayers on this melodic smooth out track. O.C. is letting you know not to be a hypocrite, pretender, or imposter in his presence. This might be the shortest song on the album, but it got me wishing for another verse.

It's Only Right/Da Beatminerz

This record just breathes hip-hop and sounds like the five or more elements. O.C. gives me the god of the emcee's presence of Rakim on this song.

Jewelz/Lord Finesse

The title track breathes a different sound before producer/rapper Lord Finesse changes the tempo to a classic D.I.T.C. sound that is as rough as the ocean. This beat bangs like a Brown Antechinus. Let's just put it this way, the album is one of my favorites and it should be

Marquis Walker

yours too. Listen, learn, enjoy, and appreciate the sounds of O.C.

Chapter 18
SITTIN' ON CHROME (MAY 1995)

Masta Ace has always been a top tier emcee that for some reason gets over-passed when hip-hop speaks on the best. I'm glad that I have a history with his music, to keep him relevant. This concept album was more than a classic; it was a movie. Now if you're looking for this album on music platforms, it's going to be under Masta Ace Incorporated, when he was in a group.

Intro/Reginaid Ellis & Norman Clover

It's when the South meets the East, and they connect with difference, culture, and adventure. His cousin is visiting for the summer, and they get into some shenanigans.

The I.N.C. Ride/Luis Vega

There are a couple of versions of this song. I believe this is the best one, with its smooth melodic funk sound allowing Mr. Ace a platform to flow like butter. This song has you repeating it from beginning to end. It's a slept-on album that gives you good vibes enough to spark up and just ride too.

Marquis Walker

Eastbound/Ase One:

As soon as the beat rides, you're hooked onto the track like a bra. From the support from the I.N.C. crew, to the Ad-libs, the song has you hypnotized. I'm on my feet sliding on my floors and going along with the song like I wrote it. "It's the I to the N to the C, you can't "F" with them!"

What's Going On! /Norman Glover, Reginald Ellis & Ase One:

The intro of the record is hilarious. It's the day of the hook-up. What he or she looks like first before we connect conversation, that usually turns uglier than a Master P sneaker.

The production on this track and the entire project is just as fire as the lyricist. Masta Ace is the main rapper on the entire album, but you will hear the crew occasionally added as either a chorus, ad-libs, or a verse.

The B-Side ft Leschea, Lord Digga & Paula Perry/Ase One

This is the actual first time you hear the crew putting in some bars. They ride the beat polished like the chrome on the whip. The group consists of Lord Digga, Paula Perry and Leschea. With the success of "Jeep Ass Niguh" & "Crooklyn" Ace returned in 1995 with this album, "Sittin' on Chrome."

And the B-side relates to when musicians used to have different versions of the record or another side to the record. This joint bumps with a West Coast influence with East Coast bars.

Sittin' on Chrome/Ase One

This song just breathes classic with the beat to the flow. From the chorus that honors the late Eazy-E from legendary group N.W.A, the song grips you and keeps your attention. Masta Ace knows how to entertain and be bar-worthy at the same time.

People in My Hood/Sean McFadden

Masta Ace says, "These are the people in my neighborhood, these are people in my neighborhood... and most of them are up to no good." Mr. Ace takes us on a tour of his hood and gives you some gossip. The hood is in disarray through his eyes, and you can tell through his rap he's not happy about it. At the end, there's a skit on the continuation of his cousin's visit that is just as funny as the previous.

Turn It Up ft Leschea/Ase One, Norman Glover & Reginald Ellis

The skit prior is when Ace and his cousin's dates want the rap music changed in the car. This is the record Ace switches the mood to, to get the women to be comfortable in the ride. Leschea's singing game is on point and she sounds a bit 90s-ish, but still pulls off the record enough to ride too. At the end of the recording, Ace is mad because his cousin is getting various calls and taking over the scene.

U Can't Find Me ft Lord Digga & Paula Perry & /Ase One

Masta Ace and Lord Digga let the world know that they are too far ahead of the rap pack, they can't find them. The beats continue to be funky, relaxing, and rideable.

Ain't No Game ft Leschea, Lord Digga & Paula Perry: Ase One

The I.N.C. rock the mic while the bass rocks and the ride is pulled over for a smoke break. They sound good as a group, and I ponder why they didn't continue to put out hits as such. And just to let you know, Ase One is Masta Ace's producer name. He's been putting work in on the boards as well as in the booth. He's one of the best rappers and producer combos.

Freestyle? /Reginald Ellis & Norman Glover

The Queen Latifah samples were tight as Masta Ace puts in a freestyle that will make you proud. Most rappers currently don't even know how to freestyle. It's a part of the culture, so it should be respected and brought forward.

Terror ft Lord Digga & Leschea/Ase One

This track is so smooth, silk is jealous. These were the times when all songs were over three minutes, and we had a better attention span. Not only can you just ride to this music, but you can also just put it on in the home and groove and move. It's one of those records that takes you on a virtual trip. At any time, Mr. Ace wants you to know he can clear out the whack rappers with his pen game.

At the end of the record Jerome, who is Ace's cousin, is on the phone and slips up with his now baby momma. The skits and storyline are that the cousin has gotten too comfortable up East and now has unbreakable relationships.

Da Answer ft Leschea/Ase One

This record speaks on the power of hip-hop music and having a good time. It's a smooth jazz track that the artist added flavor to for your ears.

4 Da Mind ft Cella Dwellas & Lord Digga/Ase One

They continue the jazz and are joined by the group Cella Dwellas putting out a quality joint record. They give you lyrics for the mind. It's from the days when groups got together and put in rap bars that they deemed to be rewindable.

Born to Roll/Ase One

This is a remix of "Jeep Ass Niguh" with that additional bass that will have the rodents moving out, from the era when you used to add additional speakers in the car that would get a cop's attention. So, turn this up and watch the paint peel from the walls. Masta Ace quotes, "I wonder if I blasted a little Elvis Presley, would they pull me over and attempt to arrest me. I really doubt doubt it, they probably start dancing, jumpin' on my tip and pissing in they pants and wiggling and jiggling and grabbing on they pelvis."

The Phat Kat Ride ft Lord Digga/Luis Vega

Artists back then did many remixes to their songs. This one is a remix from the song The I.N.C. Ride with Paula Perry on the bridge though. Which one do you crave better? They both smooth as linoleum floors. If you're not riding clean or dirty with this album by now, you may have to return your hip-hop card. It's the ride.

Chapter 19
STRICTLY BUSINESS (JUNE 1988)

Before De La Soul, EPMD was my favorite group, and you couldn't tell me anything. I tried to rap like them, dress like them and talk like them. I'm pretty sure I was telling people I was related. Let's just say I could probably mimic this entire album along with others. This debut album was released by Fresh/Sleeping Bag Records and went gold in four months. Back then, that was unheard of for rap. The entire album was produced by both Erick Sermon and PMD, better known as E-Double and Parrish Making Dollars.

Strictly Business/EPMD:
The way this album started off with their first single and title cut gets me so hyped that I start dancing and looking for a bucket hat which they made famous in the community. When I couldn't find my stupid "dookee" link with my fisherman hat, I just grabbed a hairbrush and pimp hat instead and rapped in the mirror. They have one of the best back-to-back flows to date. I'm pretty sure even Styles P and Jadakiss studied their flows.

Marquis Walker

I'm Housin'/EPMD

    This song samples "Rock Steady" by Aretha Franklin the Queen, as the Kings of Hip-Hop at the time spit some of the hardest raps without cursing. EPMD was a world premiere at the time, and you found various groups trying to imitate their style, charisma, and rhyme patterns.

Let the Funk Flow/EPMD

    This song gives me hip-hop goose bumps before they even get to the microphone. Those days rappers were feared without all the shoot 'em up bang bang songs. You enjoyed the music, danced to the music, rapped to the music, but always showed respect to the group. These were my role models back then and to this day, I respect them individually. The track was funky, and their lyrics are quotable.

You Gots to Chill/EPMD

    If you're wondering why, you need two neck braces after the track goes off, it's because they sampled "Catch a Groove" by Juice, "More Bounce to the Ounce" by Zapp & "Jungle Boogie" by Kool & the Gang - groups that had more funk in their fingers than we all have in our bodies. And you should see the list of others who sampled this song. It's longer than a test you forgot to study for.

Cevere's Chronicles Vol. 2

Shoutout to DJ K La Boss for the cuts and scratches. DJing back then was more appreciated and it's coming back to hip-hop. So, as EPMD tells you to chill in the calmest manner, you find yourself doing their dance "Steve Martin", the WAP or the Biz Mark.

It's My Thing/EPMD

Every time I hear helicopters, I think this song is about to come on and I'm ready to rap the entire thing. In my opinion, it's one of their best records - period. I've played this record more than someone on Tik-Tok trying to do the latest dance. These rappers put more than their foot in the cooking pot for seasoning. They rocked this song like no other. It has to be one of the best back-and-forth raps ever. I'm not sure who I want to imitate rapping in the mirror, so I usually put on a show and do both.

The beat is so catchy, and there's no chorus. Besides the drums when Parrish says 'Freeze' it's just bar after bars of pure heat. I'd put this song up against records now. What group goes back-to-back like this and does it well? They could have gone on for another five minutes and I would still be rocking to this record.

You're A Customer/EPMD

If you're not on your feet and moving your body, then you need to get your pulse checked. This beat is so

Marquis Walker

"funky fresh", def, and dope, it's got me writing like we are in the 1980s. They lit this song up like the 4th of July and make you want to wish you wrote this joint. We were customers to their fantastic flow, rhyme schemes and beat selections. If you're not a fan by now, we need that hip-hop card again.

The Steve Martin/EPMD

Do yawl kids think dancing moves started with you? Not in your wildest dreams, kids. Creating a dance and song that went with it is not easy. Artists tried and failed. EPMD are stamped in the record books for not just creating dance moves but starting many trends.

Get Off the Bandwagon/EPMD

The group wanted you to get off their bandwagon, but songs this good, made you want to rebel and get on their bozaks. And the bozak is equivalent to a man's privates. It's slang for getting off their package without postage. Not only did they invent dances, but they were also creating words. This group made and continues to make an impact on hip-hop.

D.J. K La Boss?

This is the DJ showing off his technique skills and splitting records with his fancy scratching styles. This is when albums are still respected for having the DJ. He was cutting it up for sure.

Jane/EPMD

This record sampled "Papa Was Too" by Joe Tex & "Mary Jane" by Rick James. The group flipped this record and made it another cultural item that rappers are still doing. This song became a saga concept and it continued to their various albums. Other rappers to this day still utilize this same formula.

It's a song about a woman who was foul in every manner. And each time they ran into her, she changed her looks and demeanor like she was James Bond or something. The records are fun, entertaining, and bring hilarious stories to the genre. What was your favorite Jane record? This started off the series of Jane records and I always wonder; will they bring Jane back?

EPMD is a legendary group that will go down in history as one of the best that's ever-done music. So, all hail Brentwood, New York Erick, and Parrish Making Dollars for their unique sound, which blends funky samples with hard-hitting beats as they lay down smooth rap deliveries and clever wordplay.

Chapter 20
STREET CINEMA (AUGUST 1998)

The group Sporty Theivz were so underrated and swept under the hip-hop rug that people only tend to remember their rebuttal to the TLC "No Scrubs" record with the "No Pigeons" version.

The Yonkers rappers brought more to the table than that. This album alone was solid and showcased lyrical prowess and unique sound. The tracks were diverse, creative, and well-crafted, and the lyrics touched on various themes such as street tales, spirituality, and just partying. This is why these soldiers will always be played in my tape box.

Intro/Unknown

The introduction describes every record as a movie of some sort. It's the guys hanging out and attending to this album in movie form. This project could even be developed into a play.

The Spot/Ski

It's a clever record about a cop and street hustler both telling their sides of the same story. The narc is planning a raid to the spot while the hustlers continue to get money. The back-to-back flow from the rappers is top tier throughout the project. Every city has a spot—a place to go to get things you want at a reasonable price. What did your spot sell?

Fedz/Freeks Skit/Ski

The Feds infiltrated the spot and now the players are on the run. This album is cinematic and movie-like with dope skits, funny skits, and a great strong structure. Who hasn't had a family member on the run? No comment.

Freeks/Slow Money Toney/Ski & King Kirk

The album gets onto a lighter note and they're speaking on the ladies who are freaky-deaky. Even gangster movies had time for freaks. They got their groove on.

Spy Hunters/Ski

We're back to the Sporty Theivz cinema as King Kirk, Big Dubez and Marlon Brando speak on their spy stories. The way they incorporated movie titles is brilliant. This album is so underappreciated that I listened to it twice for the haters who are not listening.

Like Father, Like Son/C.E.O. Freestyle/Ski

The title of the song tells the subject of the record, but the way this group rapped and developed this pro-

Marquis Walker

ject is still a highlight. Back when I was little, I knew little to nothing about what my parents did, but adults would always say to me, "You remind me of your father."

They also had some of the best transitions and skits on a project. Production hits right and their flows are on point.

Raw Footage ft Tragedy Khadafi/Ski

Track continues the filmic theme of the album while feature Tragedy joins the raw track. This was the B-Side of their lead single, "Cheapskate". This song brings things to light as you visualize the stories being told.

Hitmen/Cheapskit/King Kirk & Ski

Another clever record with the group telling visual stories about being professional hitmen. These concept records are always welcome, and the group was brilliant with them. All members could really rap.

Cheapskate/Ski

This was their first single, and it was hotter than Arizona pavement on a 100-degree day. Sounds like the group was being practical and not cheap. This song is fun, quotable, and entertaining.

Angel/Ski & King Kirk

The good and bad angel on each shoulder giving

you options on life situations. Each scenario with the group left them with decisions that were life changing. Listen to your angel and do the right thing like Spike Lee.

Mac Daddy/Aquaskit/Ski & King Kirk

The project lightens up again and its player time. Put on some clean threads, shine the Cadillac, and pick up the foxy ladies. The Mac Daddy and Daddy Mac put on a show. Another fun and entertaining song with a head-nod factor.

I believe this album and the group were missed by so many. The group had chemistry, flow, and song structure like no other.

Aqumen/King Kirk & Ski

Most records are movies in music form. The group is so talented at the story and back and forth flow. They are robbing the mob on this melodic track.

Ready ft Peter Gunz/Ski

Peter Gunz joins the crew on the chorus as they stay ready, putting in work on the mic. The track is upbeat as they add additional wordplay to their catalog.

Propose a Toast/King Kirk & Ski

This record speaks on toasting to the fallen, locked up, or struggling. It's deep and church-like and works

Marquis Walker

well with the flow of the project. Let's toast to group member Marlon Brando. He was killed by a drunk driver while walking on the sidewalk. Rest in Paradise Mr. Brando.

Street Cinema/Ski

The title record and last mini movie track just gives the group a platform to get rid of some heat. This track is dark and grimy as their lyrics match.

No Pigeons/Kevin Briggs

It's a rebuttal and parody of the legendary group TLC's, "No Scrubs". This rendition gives the man's view of the hit record. I love this record, but I always wondered if it crippled them. Most people only know them for this record, which is a shame.

Chapter 21
DIRTY HARRIET (APRIL 2000)

"Rah Digga, first name Rashia." – Rah Digga

Rah Digga aka Rashia Tashan Fisher first gained prominence in the mid-1990s with the group Flipmode Squad, which was led by the living legend Busta Rhymes. She started out with the group The Outsidaz, and no matter what group she represented, she shined. This debut album is considered a classic in underground realms, but I believe it's a classic album - period.

If you're interested in knowing more about Rah, she speaks on her career in detail on various podcasts. Hopefully, one day, she will bless mine.

Intro

One of the lieutenants of the Flipmode Squad, aka Rampage, spits some bars to introduce the queen, but at the same time letting you know he raps, too.

Harriet Thugman/Busta Rhymes

Rah Digga, aka Harriet Thugman of hip-hop, adds her own intro record and just murders the mic.

Tight/Mr. Walt

Lyrics are tight, voice box is tight, substance is tight,

and so on. Rah could write and she raps tighter than 90 percent of your favorite rappers.

Fact Checker News: She learned how to rap by studying KRS-One, Rakim and Kool G Rap while maintaining a 1300 SAT score. And she always has a composition notebook, just in case she wants to write rhymes.

What They Call Me/Pete Rock

Speaking of KRS-One, this song is, of course, paying homage to Boogie Down Productions' "By All Means Necessary" with the song sampling, "Jimmy" record. Dope remake with Pete Rock and Queen Digga Digga.

Fact Checker News: Go check her out on various other projects such as RJ Payne's "Hell's Fury", DJ Kay Slay's "Rolling 100 Deep", and Nottz "Black Woman" song.

Do the Ladies Run This ft Sonja Blade & Eve/Shok

Speaking of Black women, these three women put in some work on this record. Shoutout to Sonja Blade for sparking it off, then Eve stamping the package, then Rah Digga shutting it down.

Imperial ft Busta Rhymes/Shock

Rah Digga got lyrics to go, and she can rap with the best emcees to date. Busta Rhymes dueted on this two-step, head-bobbing track with animated bars. When they go back-to-back rapping, it strengthens the song and gives you cravings for more.

At the end of the song, they have a skit that imitates The Apollo Theatre where they boo off a country act and shoot him off the stage.

Curtains ft Lord Have Mercy/Busta Rhymes

Mr. Mercy is just on the hook while Busta handles the cold track. Rah Digga is next on the stage, and she lets people know it's curtains for these other rappers.

Showdown/Nottz

Another head-nodding track from Nottz. Rah is tighter than Ebenezer Scrooge on the mic. Rah shows and proves throughout the album she is one of the best to do this.

The Last Word ft Outsidaz/Nottz

Prior to being on Flipmode Squad, she repped the group, The Outsidaz. This is Rah Digga's other group with members: Pacewon, Nawshis, Young Zee, AZ Iziz, Slang Ton, B. Skillz, D.U., Denz, Loon One, AX and Yah Yah. Eminem and Bizarre were affiliates of the group as honorable members.

Shoutout to Nottz on the boards, giving the Outsidaz and Rah room to demolish this headbanger track.

Marquis Walker

Break Fool/Rockwilder

The battle rapping style of rapping had other emcees scared of the queen. How talented is Rah Digga? I'll answer you. Very.

Straight spittin', Pt. II/Nottz

This is one of my favorite tracks with Nottz. Rah Digga aka Dirty Harriet is spitting "Lou's" on all rappers on this joint. Rah is definitely a top-five female rapper and makes my top-25 rappers list, period.

What's Up Wit' That/Nottz

A continuation of "Head Nottzing" production from one of the best producers in the genre. Rah Digga wants and needs to know what's up with that in a gritty way. She's writing rhymes with a heavy pen game, and they're grimy at the same time.

So Cool ft Carl Thomas/Dave Atkinson

This is a R&B-ish, toe-tapping track with singer Carl Thomas lending his smooth voice to Digga's more rough vocal tone. I can hear this one in the club for sure.

Just for You ft Flipmode Squad/Nottz

The Flipmode Squad consist of Baby Cham, Lord Have Mercy, Rah Digga, Rampage, Spliff Star, and Busta Rhymes. When the group forms into Flipmode Squad, it's like Devastator on the Transformers.

F**k Ya'll N*ggas ft Young Zee/Dors'd & Ill-X

Great transition from the previous record. Rah is heated, mad, and she is clowning the n*ggas. Young Zee is also just as disrespectful on the record. It's like TLC's "No Scrubs" mixed with Sporty Thievz' "No Pigeons". I really enjoy it when Young Zee and Rah Digga rap together and wish they'd put out an album.

Lessons of Today/DJ Premier

Premo and Rah on a track? This just makes me crave more from both. Loving the track, scratches and samples used by Premier. Rah Digga's stories were impeccable, and she is also a good storyteller when she raps.

Fact Checker News: Rah Digga was supposed to release a second album in 2004 on Clive Davis' J Records, but it was shelved. Flipmode's 2nd album was also shelved.

Handle Your B.I./DJ Scratch (Bonus)

I wonder why this wasn't a regular album cut. This is an incredible collaboration with DJ Scratch.

Clap your Hands/Megahertz (Bonus)

This could have been left off the project. The song is

Marquis Walker

okay, but not as appealing as the rest of the album. The album itself is top shelf and gives me hip-hop goose bumps every year that I play it. And I play it more than once a year.

Fact Checker News: In addition to Rah Digga's music career, she's also an actress. She played in *Thirteen Ghost* and *Save the Last Dance 2.* She also played roles in hit television shows *The Wire* and *Law & Order: Special Victims Unit.* And she's still acting.

Chapter 22
STUNTS, BLUNTS, & HIP HOP (SEPTEMBER 1992)

Classic albums are never forgotten. They are played year-round, no matter what is hot on the streets. When you mention an artist's name, most people yell out their classic projects if they are lucky. Diamond D is one of those artists. This is Diamond's debut album that didn't do well commercially, but the underground scene has praised it as a classic.

The one mystery of the project everyone wonders is: who is the Psychotic Neurotics? During an interview with HipHopDX, Diamond finally answered that question. "It was my DJ KX. It was my hype man, Whiz One, and then Sha-Ease and my man Tommy; they were the dancers." Mystery solved. Now let's get into this work of art.

Intro/Diamond
It's just that; An introduction to the project.

Best Kept Secret/Diamond
The best-kept secret was that Diamond could really rap, and not just rap, but rhyme better than your favorite emcees. We already knew his production was stellar,

Marquis Walker

and now we know his raps were just as lethal. His delivery is hilarious, entertaining, lyrical, and valuable to the culture. He studied under two of the greatest lyricists, Grand Puba and Lord Finesse, who surrounded him prior to even thinking about putting out this solo work of art.

Sally Got A One Track Mind/Diamond
After finding out he could rap, he blessed us with a story that gave us 2Pac, "Brenda's Got A Baby" vibes. Another lost girl in the neighborhood went down the wrong road, and Sally, unlike Brenda, had a chance in the world. Her parents were well off, but Sally became a loose lady of the night without being on the curb. The tracks that Diamond created were cinematic.

Step To Me/Diamond & Showbiz
On this jazz-influenced groovy track, Diamond gets help on production from the legendary Showbiz from Showbiz & AG group. Again, Diamond just proves he gets busy on the microphone and welcomes rappers to step to him. It seemed like he only cursed when needed.

Shut The "*!*!" Up/Diamond
Diamond and his crew put together some hilarious and entertaining skits between these classic recordings just to break up the music. So shut the "F" Up!

"*!*!" What U Heard/Diamond & Lakim Shabazz

This record follows the funny skit and sets this up like bowling pins as Diamond dives in with lyrical fire. I enjoy the sampled chorus with Brand Nubian member Sadat X while the beat bumps in my hip-hop soul.

I'm Outta Here/Diamond

This joint bumps like Spirit Airlines and Rocky Road ice cream. It's another well-written story by Diamond about around-the-way situations. In every verse, Diamond, aka John Doe, needs another address based on the problems that occur. I played this song so many times, I've memorized it and acted it out in my mirror.

A Day In The Life ft Lord Jamar & Sadat X/Diamond

Diamond's Nubian brothers joined him on this smooth banger. As they quote, "It's just a day in the life of three Black men." And each one of them gives us a view of what they are into daily. This is a head-nodding song.

Last Car On The 2 Train/Diamond

This is another skit that brings humor through the dozens. They are playing the dozens, which just means cracking jokes.

Marquis Walker

Red Light, Green Light/Diamond

Diamond brings a childish-like game to hip-hop on this joint but puts a spin on it. This is a stop-and-go relationship record. We get a story on one of his stunts. Diamond is just not trying to get played out here in these streets.

I Went for Mine/Diamond

This beat is funkier than Rick James' jerry curls back in the day. Diamond is known for digging in the crates and finding these samples that come alive. The artist went for him on this debut album, and it all paid off. Each record has style, charisma, and flair. The album is cohesive, but each record lives on its own.

Comments From Big "L" And Showbiz

Skit is just what the title quotes. Artists Big L and Showbiz let us know real rap is back. Rest in Paradise Big L. One of the dopest on the mic.

Check One, Two/Diamond & The 45 King

With a bit of help from legend, The 45 King, Diamond puts together another song that is hotter than your breath when you wake up. So, check one, your breath. And check two, this dope song. And after you brush your gums, let me know how you feel about how Diamond took over surprisingly with this record and album.

What You Seek/Diamond

In this track, Diamond goes in and attacks the beat like it's going out of style. I would enjoy it if Diamond broke down each record with the samples and records, he used on this. I would also love to see his rhyme book in the rap museum too.

Lunchroom Chatter/Diamond

Another skit about cracking jokes on each other. Wish they were a bit longer.

Confused/Diamond

This song is a hit like the 1970's skating rinks. Diamond jumps right in and gives us another classic record that involved an ex-girlfriend that wanted to get back in his life after he got on his feet. He's confused about whether to take her back or not. I've been through this a couple of times in my life. I never took any ex-girlfriends back. Are you in a confused situation?

Pass Dat S**T ft Whiz One, Maestro Fresh Wes, Mike Q & Fat Joe/Diamond

This Posse cut that is meant to sound like a Cypher around the lunch table hits just right. Every rapper put in some work, and this is one of the first times you hear the legend, Fat Joe. It sounded like each rapper was hungry on the microphone. It made the song sound

Marquis Walker

gritty, fresh, and just with the times.

Freestyle (Yo, That's The Sh...)/Diamond & The Large Professor

With the help of legend, The Large Professor, Diamond put together another headbanger that you turn up until the police come. I always wondered if this was really one of his freestyles. No matter if it is or not, it's a standout cut that hit you in the gut and gives you hip-hop goose bumps.

K.I.S.S. (Keep It Simple Stupid)/Diamond & Q-Tip

I hear Q-Tips influence in this track, and it has A Tribe Called Quest vibe. Rest in Paradise Phife. Either way, Diamond kicks a hole in this speaker and adds more quality rap to his pages. So, kiss the ring.

Fact Checker News: Did you hear that A Tribe Called Quest and Outkast were going to put out an album?

Stunts, Blunts, & Hip Hop/Diamond

The title cut is saved until the end of the record. Now, Diamond gives us evaluations on each topic. Stunts are women, blunts are the cigars they use to smoke weed in, and of course, Hip Hop is the culture that Diamond breaks down and gives credit to.

Cevere's Chronicles Vol. 2

Wuffman Stressed Out/Diamond

A quick skit of Wuffman Jack talking trash. Don't ask me why this is even on the project. It brings humor.

Feel The Vibe ft Showbiz/Diamond

Diamond brings some jazz and funk to this joint, while rapper Showbiz finally joins the party. The record is cool enough to not be skipped, sounds dated, but still brings character to the project.

A View from the Underground/Diamond

They end with Fat Joe the gangster just talking that talk.

Diamond D is known for saying, "I'm the best producer on the mic." With this debut album and various projects that came after, in my book, he's one of them. Many have come after, but Diamond is one of the forefathers of producing and emceeing his own classics. This project, "Stunts, Blunts & Hip Hop" is a masterpiece that stands the test of time, and I'd put it up there with whatever you bring to the table.

Chapter 23
MOMENT OF TRUTH (MARCH 1998)

Let's speak on the obvious, first. Rest easy Guru, aka Keith, who passed away on April 19, 2010. It seems like yesterday that you were here with us, giving us the right tools to get through this difficult world.

Gang Starr is one of the best Hip-Hop groups to-date, and nothing can discredit their title. They will be in the top-five group ranking, period, and will live on to be studied on how to do it best. With DJ Premier's digging in the crates, DJ skills and masterful beat making, and Guru's intriguing, incredible, and outstanding emceeing, we have classic material. If you're not aware, DJ Premier produced every track on this project.

You Know My Steez

Guru starts off schooling a reporter at the beginning of the song about how the group Gang Starr keeps it real and right. Once the beat rocks, we are heavily reminiscent of how great a producer/DJ Premier is. Baldhead Slick, aka Guru, spoke correctly with the reporter because he always brought substance, entertainment, and new flavor.

Robbin Hood Theory

The Robin Hood theory in the fictional writings, they stole from the rich and gave to the poor. I believe Guru gave back jewels to the hood once he learned them. When he learned something relevant, he made sure he put it on wax over one of Premo's dope beats.

Work

DJ Premo and Guru's workload was always appreciated, and they put in overtime in that studio. This track got me bobbing my head, dancing, and learning at the same time. This combination created history, and victory is theirs.

Royalty ft K-Ci & JoJo

This track sounds like Royalty while portions of the group Jodeci put on a smooth chorus. Guru's monotone voice box continues to give us a clear and consistent feeling. With Premo creating these tracks and adding significant scratching throughout, the songs continue to sound fresh as organic produce. At the end of the record, Premo goes in on these sucker producers because Guru already took care of the sucker emcees.

Above the Clouds ft Inspectah Deck

This is another solid record from DJ Premiere that gives you hip-hop goose bumps. The beat bangs like

Marquis Walker

your favorite porn stars. Feature Inspectah Deck comes through and adds additional value and puts a dent in the left speaker as Guru chokes out the right. Deck is top three to me when it comes to the Wu-Tang member's period.

JFK 2 LAX

From one part of America to the other, Gang Starr locked up the ears of hip-hop culture. This song is a true story as Guru gets held up and goes through his lawyer to get back on track. Music allows you to realize that these artists are human and go through trials and tribulations, just like us.

Itz A Set Up ft Hannibal

Another hard-hitting record with that bass that will shake the windows. Feature, Hannibal, sounds good, but like Freddie Foxx with less grit. Guru has one of the smoothest flows, no matter who joins the track.

Fact Checker News: Guru stands for Gifted Unlimited Rhymes Universal.

Moment of Truth

The title song has a great universal sound and gives you a relaxing tone while Guru speaks on Karma. Everyone will meet their moment of truth. It's good and evil out here. Which will you honor the most? It's known that it's easier to be bad than good, and smiling takes more muscles to create. It's all about the energy you decide to use.

B.I. Vs. Friendship ft M.O.P.

If you don't know by now, business and friendship can go left, and Guru is just reminding us. With features, Billy, and Fame, coming through, this may be an exception. This track comes together like your favorite movie. It always seems like the Mash Out Posse takes over a record with their distinctive aggressive style. They do, but in a good way.

The Militia ft Big Shug & Freddie Foxx

This is another stand-out song that rocks like the 1970s. This track sounds like it just used cocaine and speed at the same time. This is one of my favorite songs on the project. It just gives me enough energy to build a home from scratch. Shug and Foxx are hyper than pop rocks candy and soda mixed, and you would think louder artists would blow Guru out of the box, but they just don't. Freddie Foxx was the highlight of the record though.

Marquis Walker

The Rep Growz Bigga

The introduction of the record has a young lady checking a couple of people. She said, "You can give me head till I'm dead." Lol. Then Premo and Guru get back to work with some clever raps about having a good representation and a track that allows him to do so. I always love it when DJ Premier takes over on the scratches. It never gets old.

What I'm Here 4

The piano-driven track allows Guru, aka Jazzmattaz, to speak to us in teacher mode. I've always enjoyed his point of view while Premo's beats made us want to bang our heads off the wall.

Fact Checker News: Keith Edward Elam was born in Roxbury, Massachusetts.

She Know What She Wantz

The mellow jazz track gives the rapper a platform to speak on the Black Queen Widow knowing what she wants. It gives us a chance to peep at the rapper's versatility on the microphone as he speaks about a particular lady in his life in the second verse. There's nothing wrong with knowing what you want.

Cevere's Chronicles Vol. 2

New York Strait Talk

Big Shug explaining how Gang Starr started in Boston and had to take it to New York to get that deal. If y'all don't know, there still aren't any major opportunities for Boston artists. Guru was smart to venture off and make it in NYC. DJ Premo put his foot in this beat and scratched with classic samples from EPMD.

My Advice 2 You

The Professor Guru spoke various good messages on these records without sounding preachy. He was like a mix of Chuck D and Flavor Flav. The bars were quotable and relatable to the masses, which I still honor.

Make 'Em Pay ft Krumb Snatcha

If you are still reading, I commend you. This generation doesn't have a large attention span. These albums are three-times longer than what is expected today for albums. The combination of DJ Premier and Guru took us on a long ride that kept us interested the entire ride. Shoutout to Krumb Snatcha from Boston with the fire verse.

The Mall ft G-Dep & Shiggy Sha

As soon as you believe the album was going to settle with just pure hip-hop music, DJ Premo spices it up a bit. This track is up-tempo and gives the rappers a fun

Marquis Walker

record to shop their lyrics. Rest in Paradise to G-Dep.

Betrayal ft Scarface

This song alone is longer than some of these artists' EP's. Premo slows down the tempo while Guru and Facemob rap about untrustworthy members of society. This track sounds like it would be on a Scarface album too. I'm sure Premo did that on purpose. Shoutout to Scarface who is one of my favorite rappers, period. This is a rewindable record and the legend, Face, stamped the package. It's No Justice, Just Us.

Next Time

It's better luck next time when it comes to this dynamic duo. The incredible beats that fed Guru's hungry verses made the energy in the room just right.

In Memory of...:

They end the record in memory of the ones they loved and continue to love. Let's add in memory of Guru to the top of the list. Wish he was still around handing us moments of truth. To all reading, in memory of your loved ones as well.

Chapter 24

Hell on Earth (November 1996)

We are going to Queensbridge to visit another top-five hip-hop group, Mobb Deep. Rest in Paradise to Prodigy, half of the infamous mobb. Some say this album is better than their second album, "The Infamous". I love them both and believe an artist/group can have more than one classic project.

Animal Instinct ft Ty Nitty & Gambino

They start off the project hotter than grits down south. You must wonder what kind of air they were inhaling while making these records. This one starts off letting you know they haven't taken their foot off the pedals. It's full speed ahead with the street bars, boom bap beat, and great features to compliment the Mobb.

Drop A Gem On 'Em

Just when you ask if this album is going to be all fire, they drop this gem on us. When this beat came on, the murder rate elevated to 90%. Prodigy was dissing Tupac on this track if you must know. I'm pretty sure they are both laughing it up in Hip-Hop Heaven now. This track is quotable and makes you just want to do crime.

Marquis Walker

Bloodsport

The track sounds simple but classic. Production on this album improved from their previous albums and was highlighted throughout our speakers. Havoc and Prodigy's classic voice boxes that carried the streets through their tales just added more pressure to all rap groups in the 1990s. They were spitting that trife life.

Extortion ft Method Man

After each song, I would think there's no way they can keep it going, but I would continuously hear tracks like this. Doesn't Method Man know how to select some of the hottest beats to be on? He must have a magnetic vibe to dope tracks. Meth was extorting these artists to get on these killer tracks.

More Trife Life

Instead of making this part two, they just gave us more trife life stories from the Queensbridge projects. The stories were always negative energy with positive messages if you're in those situations. It's like Mobb warned all thugs on what not to do because it just happened to them. Havoc's storytelling is top-notch and should be spoken about.

Man Down ft Big Noyd

Havoc had some of the most gritty, dangerous, and

dark tracks to go with their flows. With the third Mobb member, Big Noyd, who was always welcomed, they took these songs to the hood promise lands. They were literally laying men down through their verses.

Fact Checker News: The group, the Beatnuts, sampled this on their record, "Hammer Time".

Can't Get Enough of It ft General G

More glorious production from Havoc. He should be spoken about more for Producer/Rapper combinations. He's somehow forgotten about when hip-hop speaks about artists that mastered both. Shoutout to feature General G for blessing the song. This record is underestimated and not talked about enough.

Nighttime Vultures ft Raekwon

This track always hits me over the head and speaks of NYC to the fullest. The music just puts fear in the air as high as the crows flying on the record. Another Wu Member joins the Mobb, putting out some dope bars. The purple tape General Rae always comes through with his own "dun" language. This is another banging song that carries this project.

Marquis Walker

G.O.D. Pt. III

Even the skits are classic on this joint. The busting out the window is iconic while the Twilight theme rings in the background. The music was just organically on top of the world, and it was like every beat was fighting each other. The dark, gritty, and cinematic track just sounds like a movie score while the group speaks gangster making all Godfathers proud.

Get Dealt With

This track may take a bit of a break on the speakers, but the sounds are still matching their heavy street lyrics that carry over. Mobb's chemistry is one of the best, and if you are speaking of your favorite groups, they must be in the top five, guaranteed.

Hell on Earth (Front Lines)

Just when you thought the Mobb was slowing down and running out of firecracker sounds, they develop this. They kept their competition in the back and stayed on the front lines. This is another great record that is internationally known, and I'm sure aliens rock, as well. Music, as such, doesn't even have to be understood, and creatures are quoting this all day and night.

Fact Checker News: Various other artists sampled this record. EPMD, Beanie Sigel, Planet Asia, Erykah Badu,

Cevere's Chronicles Vol. 2

Westside Gunn, Saigon, Bahamadia, Jedi Mind Tricks, Rakim, and more.

Give It Up Fast ft Nas & Big Noyd

This beat is just P.I.M.P. It slaps the ears like Will Smith smacked Chris Rock at the 2022 Oscars Awards. Queensbridge features unite for another hip-hop banger to add to the culture. Nas and Noyd are always a great highlight on a Mobb Deep project.

Still Shinin'

This track sounds like some evil choir at a church while the team corrupts everyone at the pulpit with these real, but foul lyrics. Song samples, "Hospital Prelude of Love Theme" by Willie Hutch.

Apostle's Warning

Track samples, "People Make the World Go Round" by Michael Jackson, believe it or not. Can you imagine Mr. Jackson singing this? Lol. Loud Records had a diamond in the rough when it came to this group. Mobb Deep's music needed two warnings on each album cover. One for the lyrics/content and the other for these killer tracks.

CHAPTER 25
SOMETHIN' TO BLAZE TO (JANUARY 1994)

I didn't put this book together with too much planning, but it seemed to be writing itself with the selections of albums. Now, this is the first Cevere's Classic Chronicles and will not be the last. So, if your classic project did not appear, don't worry, and if you would like to share yours, find me on social media and we can talk about yours possibly going into the next book.

I put this book together to honor some classic albums you've heard of and some that may surprise you. I'm pretty sure this last one is a total surprise to most. But if you know me or underground hip-hop, this is a sleeper to most, but people reading this will understand the pick after really listening to this album.

I start off the book with CMW who doesn't curse one bit, and I end it with a group that curses like it's going out of style. I would ask you to really listen to the group and give them a chance, and that goes with all the other albums I believe are classics. Thanks in advance. We are going to Flint, Michigan to highlight these gentlemen, Top Authority. They are Flex, Shotgun, and Dalo who is the producer.

Another Murda

This song is almost seven minutes long and keeps my attention through the content, flow, and sonic waves, and almost hypnotizing music. As you listen, the song continues to just get better and better. The song reminds me of a book by Kody Scott, *Monster: The Autobiography of an L.A. Gang Member*. That book is an interesting read, but long and entertaining like this song.

No Love (9mm Remix)

"Tell it to my nine!" and "Flex the Problem Solver", ring through my ears whenever this track appears. The chorus is catchy and threatening, but this head-nodding track is smooth like butter and gives you good vibes.

Money

The samples and beat and topic make this record breathtaking. We are speaking about what America runs on, and I'm not talking about donuts—that money and power. This is car riding music, gangster music, and music that makes you think. It may sound disturbing to the ears, but this is what America created at the end of the day. I believed artists took this opportunity to turn a negative into a positive to create and get paid for it.

Pussy Ain't Worth No Cash

If you have sensitive ears when it comes to the la-

Marquis Walker

dies, I'd advise you to skip this track. They are giving out graphic messages as usual, but only speaking to a small percentage of women on this planet. I agree with their message, just not their delivery. But when I was younger, I was quoting this song out loud and proud.

On the Level

This is another gangster record that killed more people than N.W.A. on their records. These songs just sound more realistic though. The music gives you chills and makes you think twice about being a gangster, which could work in your favor if you're trying to scare the kids.

Pop Him

There are so many Quotables on this track. It's a rewindable track for me. The album is so graphic, but I listen to it at least four times a year. "I had to pop 'em, I had to pop 'em!" This music may be too graphic for anyone these days, but this song is so tough. Flex says, "A bulletproof vest might stop a wound to the chest, but not the fuckin' head." They challenged the devil on this song and won. They are killing the KKK on this joint. There's some good in these records after all.

93 (Thangs Ain't How They Should Be)

The gangsters take a quick break with the "kill kill"

tracks. This record is smooth, and you can play this at the barbecue. They are speaking about the city of Flint, Michigan on the day-to-day operations. But even on the R&Bish track, things still pop off. R.I.P to the lost.

Somethin' to Blaze To

This is the title track, and it has a fun beat to it. Basically, the Flint Michigan anthem. Another smooth groove to blaze to. So, spark up and "puff puff" and don't pass. We must add this to all the other weed-smoking tracks that are classics. "Blaze it up my Nigga!"

How Much

This is another incredible, almost seven-minute track that is their "F" the police record, their "F" white people record, and even "F" Brown-on-Brown violence record. It's their wake-up record to the world. Dalo's production throughout this entire project must be praised. They ask the important question of how much can a Black person take. I ask myself that every day. It's like their gangster political record with revolutionary messages.

Voices

This beat makes you just want to pick up the heat and go make some bodies cold. Especially with this hypnotizing track making you hear voices. Rapper Shotgun

Marquis Walker

says, "cause I'm missing all my screws, G, hearing voices in my head had me grabbing for that uzi". If you're hearing voices, please go get professional help. If not, bump this record until you do hear voices. This track is on fire.

Never Leave Home Without It

The 1990s were rough for the murder rate around America. We can speak of who's to blame, but when you're at war, never leaving home without your steal, was the way to go. It was easy to get this music, too. My parents didn't monitor anything I listened to. I purchased 99.9% of my music. I was listening to music like this, but always balancing it with something like Stevie Wonder or something light. Gangster or not, this music is good. The key is what you do with it.

Half Deck (Outro)

This last track ends the album as gangster as the first record. While Flex and Shotgun collect bodies with each verse, producer Dalo keeps us interested with the production. The tracks are something to blaze to, and the street poetry is something to break down and analyze based on the period they created it. The 1990s were rough. This generation doesn't live half of what was lived during the 1990's, but for some reason, the crime rate is still bad. These kids aren't even outside. They are getting killed for having computer fingers that lead to trigger fingers. Let's not blame the music though. It's all about the environment and teachings of these children and even adults.

www.ingramcontent.com/pod-product-compliance
Lightning Source LLC
Chambersburg PA
CBHW071500080526
44587CB00014B/2166